JAPANESE
FOR
EVERYONE

JAPANESE GRAMMAR &
CONVERSATION IN 90 DAYS

JAPANESE
FOR
EVERYONE

JAPANESE GRAMMAR & CONVERSATION IN 90 DAYS

M. RAJENDRAN

Pelanduk
Publications

Published by
Pelanduk Publications (M) Sdn. Bhd.,
24 Jalan 20/16A, 46300 Petaling Jaya,
Selangor Darul Ehsan, Malaysia.

All correspondence to:
Pelanduk Publications (M) Sdn. Bhd.,
P.O. Box 8265, 46785 Kelana Jaya,
Selangor Darul Ehsan, Malaysia.

Originally published as JAPANESE GRAMMAR & CONVERSATION IN 90 DAYS

ISBN 967-978-074-0

1st printing 1985
2nd printing 1986
3rd printing 1987
4th printing 1988
5th printing 1990
6th and 7th printing 1991
8th printing 1992
9th printing 1994
10th printing 1995
11th printing 1996

Printed by
Eagle Trading Sdn. Bhd.

The Author

M. RAJENDRAN is an associate professor of Japanese history at the History Department of University Malaya, Kuala Lumpur. He is also the coordinator of the Special Japanese Programme at University Malaya's Pusat Asasi.

He obtained his Bachelor of Arts with Honours from University Malaya; his Master of Arts from Nagoya University, Japan and Ph.D. from Griffith University, Australia.

Dr. Rajendran is also the author of the highly acclaimed and authoritative MALAY-JAPANESE-ENGLISH DICTIONARY.

Contents

Isinya

PREFACE

Although tremendous interest over Japan has been generated in recent years, there is still a great dearth of materials on the Japanese language. To understand Japan and the Japanese people, knowledge of her language is an indispensable requirement. This book has been written to fulfil this need.

It is essentially a Japanese language proficiency course specially designed for native speakers of Malay or English who have negligible background in the language.

The book begins with an introduction to Japanese phonetics, written without the usual formidable terminology. After that the language structure and contents are systematically presented through a series of graded lessons. The lessons have been carefully selected to represent a wide range of topics, reflecting the spoken and written aspects of the language and its grammar. The lessons and the related topics are developed gradually, starting with the simpler and moving on to the more difficult.

Each lesson begins with an account of the common words, phrases and sentences related to a particular topic. This is followed by notes on grammar, consolidation exercises and a glossary of the items covered in that lesson.

Revision exercises have been included between lessons to evaluate the reader's understanding and acquisition of the skills taught. Answers are given for all exercises.

The innovative topic-based approach written in jargon-free style should make this book highly commendable to businessmen, tourists, students, civil servants and Japanese visitors to this country. In short, for anyone aspiring to gain a basic introduction to the Japanese language within a short period of time.

The Publisher

KATA PENGANTAR

Buku ini adalah buku yang pertama sekali ditulis di rantau ini. Buku ini diterbitkan selaras dengan kekurangan yang didapati dalam penulisan buku-buku Tatabahasa dan perbualan Jepun dalam Bahasa Malaysia. Dengan tujuan membantu dan memudahkan mereka yang tidak mempunyai pengetahuan praktikal dalam Bahasa Malaysia, saya juga telah memasukkan Bahasa Inggeris sebagai satu media tambahan, justeru menjadikan buku ini berbentuk 'trilingual'. Oleh kerana buku ini bercita-cita memberi satu kursus lengkap bagi mereka yang berminat dalam memperolehi pengetahuan asas dalam tatabahasa serta bahasa perbualan Jepun, saya telah secara tegasnya menggunakan ejaan roman.

Dalam buku ini saya telah cuba memaparkan satu susunan struktur asas dan perbendaharaan kata dalam cara yang paling mudah dan sistematik. Lantas, setiap pelajaran telah disusurgalurkan dalam satu bentuk yang seragam. Setiap pelajaran bermula dengan keterangan-keterangan tatabahasa, latihan dan perbendaharaan kata di mana setiap satu darinya direkabentukkan untuk membantu saudara dan saudari mempraktik apa yang dikehendaki oleh pelajaran itu.

Adalah dinasihatkan supaya saudara dan saudari mengulangkaji sedalam-dalamnya setiap pelajaran yang telah diberi.

Akhirkata, saya berharap agar buku ini akan menjadi asas bagi banyak lagi buku yang akan diterbitkan pada masa-masa akan datang demi mengukuhkan lagi polisi kerajaan iaitu "Dasar pandang ke Timur".

Phonetics

Japanese phonetics is monosyllabic and for some syllables there are no precise sounds. Below are some of the commonly used vowels and consonants in Japanese which are similar to those in English and Bahasa Malaysia.

Vowels		English	Bahasa Malaysia
'a'	like the vowel in	car	baik
		fan	patung
'e'	like e in	men	esok
		met	enak
'i'	like ee in	need	itik
		feet	bising
'o'	similar to o in	gone	orang
		north	oren
'u'	similar to u in	put	hutang
	(but with lips not rounded)	bush	ular

Please note that the vowels 'i' and 'u' are generally whispered or not pronounced at all.
Example: a) mimasu is pronounced as mimas
     b) imashita is pronounced as imasta

Consonants

The consonants b, k, m, n, p and w are pronounced as in English.

Consonants		English	Bahasa Malaysia
'g'	is pronounced as in	give	goreng
		go	gila
's'	is pronounced as in	see	sireh
		sir	sembilan
'sh'	is pronounced as in	ship	syair
'z'	is pronounced as in	zinc	dzuhur

't'	is pronounced as in	gets	terima
'ch'	is pronounced as in	cherry	cempedak
'j'	is pronounced as in	jeer	jaring
'm'	is pronounced as in	mother	mari
'h'	before the vowel **a, e** is pronounced as in	hop	hodoh
'w'	is pronounced as in	watch	warna
'y'	is pronounced as in	yellow	yang

Please note that consonant 'f' which occurs before u, is pronounced with lips closed together.

Also note that between voiceless consonants k, p, s, t, h *or* after voiceless consonants at the end of a phrase:

'g' is pronounced as in English — **go**
'n' is pronounced as in English — **no**
's' is always pronounced as in 'see'
'w' is pronounced with lips not rounded but left slack.

Petua-petua Fonetik

Fonetik Jepun adalah sukukata tunggal dan bagi sebahagian, sukukata tidak ada bunyi yang khusus.

Sebagai panduan disenaraikan di bawah beberapa vokal dan konsonan yang sering digunakan dalam Bahasa Jepun yang juga mempunyai persamaan ketara dalam Bahasa Inggeris dan Bahasa Malaysia.

Bunyi-bunyi vokal	Bahasa Malaysia	Bahasa Inggeris
'a' seperti vokal dalam perkataan	baik pada	car star
'e' seperti e dalam perkataan	elok esok	ten met
'i' seperti ee dalam per-kataan	itik ikan	beat eat
'o' seperti o dalam per-kataan	orang otak	gone north
'u' seperti u dalam per-kataan	udang ular	put bush

Sila perhatikan vokal 'i' dan 'u' pada umumnya dibisik atau tidak disebut langsung.

Umpamanya:
(a) mimasu disebut mimas
(b) imashita disebut imasta

Bunyi-bunyi Konsonan

Konsonan b, k, m, n, p dan w adalah sama sebutannya seperti Bahasa Inggeris.

Konsonan-konsonan	Bahasa Malaysia	Bahasa Inggeris
'g' disebut seperti dalam perkataan	garis gila	go gore

's' disebut seperti dalam perkataan	siram salam	see sea
'sy' disebut seperti dalam perkataan	syawal syair	ship shield
'dz' (pengaruh Arab) disebut seperti dalam perkataan	dzuhur zuriat	zinc zoo
't' disebut seperti dalam perkataan	tulis tumbuk	gets tell
'ch' disebut seperti dalam perkataan	cantik cantum	cherry cheap
'j' disebut seperti dalam perkataan	jaring jendela	jeer jeep
'm' disebut seperti dalam perkataan	makan malam	mother marry
'h' sebelum vokal a, e dan o disebut seperti dalam perkataan	hitam hodoh hari	hop heal hat
'w' disebut seperti dalam perkataan	wanita warna	watch
'y' disebut seperti dalam perkataan	yang	yellow

'sy' dan 'dz' adalah pengaruh Arab dalam Bahasa Malaysia.

Sila perhatikan bahawa konsonan 'f' yang wujud sebelum 'u' mestilah disebut dengan bibir yang dirapatkan.

Perhatikan juga bunyi-bunyi sebelum konsonan-konsonan tak bersuara k, p, s, t, h *atau* selepas konsonan-konsonan bersuara iaitu di hujung frasa (rangkai kata):

'g' disebut (seperti dalam perkataan Bahasa Malaysia) 'goreng'
'n' disebut (seperti dalam perkataan Bahasa Malaysia) 'nobat'
's' disebut (seperti dalam perkataan Bahasa Malaysia) 'silam'
'w' disebut dengan bibir tidak dibundarkan tapi dibiarkan terhampar.

Daiikka - Nihon go no onsetsu
Pelajaran 1 – Sukukata-sukukata Jepun
Lesson 1 – Japanese syllables

Terdapat lima vokal dasar dalam bahasa Jepun. Ia adalah a, i, u, e, o. Sukukata dasar adalah seperti berikut. Harus diperhatikan bahawa konsonan 'n' sahajalah yang boleh digunakan sebagai satu sukukata yang tersendiri.

There are five basic vowels in the Japanese language. These are a, i, u, e, o. The basic syllables are found below. It should be noted that 'n' is the only consonant that can be used in isolation.

a	i	u	e	o
ka	ki	ku	ke	ko
sa	shi	su	se	so
	(si)			
ta	chi	tsu	te	to
	(ti)	(tu)		
na	ni	nu	ne	no
ha	hi	fu	he	ho
		(hu)		
ma	mi	mu	me	mo
ya		yu		yo
ra	ri	ru	re	ro
wa				o
n				

Terdapat juga sukukata-sukukata lain yang diperolehi dari sukukata-sukukata ini dengan menggunakan suara konsonan seperti ga dari ka dan sebagainya: ataupun dengan mencantumkan dua sukukata untuk dijadikan satu seperti ki + ya = kya. Satu senarai lengkap vokal dan sukukata diberikan di bawah ini. Ini adalah seperti berikut:

There are also other syllables that are derived from these, either by voicing of consonants e.g. **ga** from **ka** etc. or by combining two syllables to form one, e.g. **ki** + **ya** = **kya**. These are as follows:

ga	gi	gu	ge	go
za	zi	zu	ze	zo
	(ji)			
da	di	du	de	do
	ji	zu		
ba	bi	bu	be	bo
pa	pi	pu	pe	po

kya	kyu	kyo
gya	gyu	gyo
sha	shu	sho
(sya)	(syu)	(syo)
ja	ju	jo
(zya)	(zyu)	(zyo)
cha	chu	cho
(tya)	(tyu)	(tyo)
nya	nyu	nyo
hya	hyu	hyo
bya	byu	byo
pya	pyu	pyo
mya	myu	myo
rya	ryu	ryo

Dainika – Nichijō Kaiwa
Pelajaran 2 – Perbualan Harian
Lesson 2 – Daily Conversation

1. **Hai.**
   Yes.

   Ya.

2. **Iie.**
   No.

   Tidak.

3. **Ohayō gozaimasu.**
   Good morning.

   Selamat pagi.

4. **Konnichi wa.**
   Good afternoon.

   Selamat tengahari.

5. **Konban wa.**
   Good evening.

   Selamat petang.

6. **Oyasumi nasai.**
   Good night.

   Selamat malam.

7. **Arigatō gozaimasu.**
   Thank you.

   Terima kasih.

8. **Dōitashi mashite.**
   Please don't mention.

   Sama-sama.

9. **Ogenki desu ka?**
   Ikaga desu ka?
   How are you?

   Apa khabar?

10. **Hai, genki desu, domo arigatō.**
    Fine, thank you.

    Baik, terima kasih.

11. **Anata wa do desu ka?**
    What about you?

    Macam mana dengan awak?

4

12. **Irasshai mase.**
Welcome.

Selamat datang.

13. **Dōzo haite kudasai.**
Dōzo ohairi kudasai.
Please enter.
Please come in.

Sila masuk.

14. **Dōzo suwate kudasai.**
Dōzo okake kudasai.
Please sit down.

Sila duduk.

15. **Dōzo kochirae.**
This way, please.

Sila ikut jalan ini.

16. **Chotto matte kudasai.**
Shōshō omachi kudasai.
Just a moment, please.

Sila tunggu sebentar.

17. **Omatase shimashita.**
Sorry to keep you waiting.

Minta maaf kerana lewat.

18. **Dō shimashita ka?**
What is the matter (with you)?

Apa hal (dengan awak)?

19. **Dare desu ka?**
Donata desu ka?
Who is it?

Siapa itu?

20. **Nan desu ka?**
What is it?

Apa itu?

21. **Doko desu ka?**
Where is it?

Di mana itu?

22. **Itsu desu ka?**
When is it?

Bila?

23. **Dochira desu ka?**
Which is it?

Yang mana?

24. **Naze desu ka?**
    Doshite desu ka?
    Why is it so?

    Kenapa begitu?

25. **Honto desu ka?**
    Is it true?

    Adakah benar?

26. **Honto ja arimasen.**
    It is not true.

    Ia tidak benar.

27. **Anata wa hima desu ka?**
    Ohima desu ka?
    Are you free?

    *Adakah anda mempunyai masa
    lapang?*

28. **Anata wa isogashii desu ka?**
    Oisogashii desu ka?
    Are you busy?

    Adakah anda sibuk?

29. **Hajimemashite. Watashi wa
    Taro desu. Dōzo yoroshiku.**
    I am Taro. I am glad to meet
    you.

    *Saya Taro. Saya gembira kerana
    dapat bertemu dengan anda.*

30. **Kochira koso, dōzo yoroshiku?**
    How do you do?

    Apa khabar?

31. **Omedetō gozaimasu.**
    Congratulations.

    Tahniah.

32. **Tanjōbi omedetō.**
    Happy Birthday.

    Selamat hari jadi.

33. **Shinen omedetō gozaimasu.**
    Happy New Year.

    Selamat Tahun Baru.

34. **Kurisumasu omedetō gozai-
    masu.**
    Merry Christmas.

    Selamat Hari Krismas.

35. **Dipavari omedetō gozaimasu.**
    Happy Deepavali.

    Selamat Hari Deepavali.

36. **Hari Raya omedetō gozai-**   *Selamat Hari Raya.*
    masu.
    Happy Hari Raya.

37. **Onaji desu.**   *Ia adalah sama.*
    It is the same.

38. **Onaji ja arimasen.**   *Ia tidak sama.*
    It is not the same.

39. **Chigaimasu.**   *Ia adalah salah.*
    It is wrong.

40. **Mada desu.**   *Belum lagi.*
    Not yet.

Bunpō   *Tatabahasa*
Grammar

1. (a) **"Desu"**   *"Desu" adalah sama dengan*
      It is similar to "is", "are",   *"ialah", "adalah" dan*
      "am" etc. in English.   *sebagainya dalam Bahasa Inggeris.*

      Watashi wa sensei desu.   *Saya seorang guru.*
      I **am** a teacher.

      Kono hito wa gakusei desu.   *Orang ini seorang pelajar.*
      This person **is** a student.

   (b) **"Ja arimasen"**   *Negatif "desu" adalah "ja*
      The negative of "desu".   *arimasen". Ia menandakan*
      It denotes "not" in English.   *"tidak" dalam Bahasa Inggeris.*

      Watashi wa sensei ja   *Saya bukan seorang guru.*
      arimasen.
      I am not a teacher.

      Sono hito wa gakusei ja   *Orang itu bukan pelajar.*
      arimasen.
      That person is not a
      student.

2. (a) **"Ka"**
"Ka" denotes a question.

"Ka" menandakan pertanyaan.

Anata wa sensei desu ka?
Are you a teacher?

Adakah anda seorang guru?

Ogenki desu ka?
How are you?

Apa khabar?

(b) **"Ka"** also denotes **Alternative Questions.**

"Ka" juga menandakan "soalan alternatif".

Anata wa sensei desu ka, gakusei desu ka?

Adakah anda seorang guru atau pelajar?

A. **Mijikai Kaiwa.**
Satu perbualan pendek.
A Short Conversation.

A: **Ogenki, desu ka?**
B: **Hai, genki desu, domo arigatō.**
   Okage sama de genki desu.
   Anata wa do desu ka?

A: **Hai, genki desu, domo arigatō.**
B: **Taro sensei wa genki desu ka?**

A: **Hai, ---**
B: **Anata wa isogashii desu ka?**

A: **Hai, ---**
   Iie, ---
B: **Kore wa pen desu ka?**

A: **Hai, ---**
   Iie, ---

A: **Anata no hon desu ka?**
B: **Hai, ---**
   Iie, ---

B. Match the following.   *Padankan yang berikut.*

1. *Selamat pagi.*   **Omedetō.**
   Good morning.

2. *Selamat tengahari.*   **Ohāyo gozaimasu.**
   Good afternoon.

3. *Selamat petang.*   **Shinen omedetō gozaimasu.**
   Good evening.

4. *Apa khabar?*   **Dōitashi mashite.**
   How are you?

5. *Tahniah.*   **Konnichi wa.**
   Congratulations.

6. *Selamat Tahun Baru.*   **Ogenki desu ka?**
   Happy New Year.

7. *Selamat malam.*   **Konban wa.**
   Good night.

8. *Sama-sama.*   **Oyasumi nasai.**
   Please don't mention.

C. *Isikan tempat-tempat kosong.*
   Fill in the blanks.

1. Anata _____ gakusei desu _____?

2. Hai, watashi _____ gakusei _____ .

3. Iie, watashi _____ gakusei _____ _____ .

4. Ano hito wa sensei _____ _____, gakusei _____ _____?

5. Shinen _____ gozaimasu.

Hombun Glossary	*Perbendaharaan Kata*
1. **Watashi** I	*Saya*
2. **Watashi no** My, mine	*Saya, kepunyaan saya*
3. **Watashi tachi** We	*Kita*
4. **Anata** You	*Anda*
5. **Anata no** Your, Yours	*Anda (kepunyaan)*
6. **Anata tachi, Anata gata** All of you, you all	*Kamu semua*
7. **Kare** He	*Dia (lelaki)*
8. **Kanojo** She	*Dia (perempuan)*
9. **Dare** Who	*Siapa*
10. **Itsu** When	*Bila*
11. **Nan** What	*Apa*
12. **Dochira** Which	*Yang mana*

13. **Naze**
Why

Mengapa

14. **Naze nara**
Because

Kerana

15. **Hai**
Yes

Ya

16. **Iie**
No

Tidak

17. **Sō**
So

Jadi

18. **Sō desu ka?**
Is it so?

Adakah begitu?

19. **Mō**
Also, already

Juga, sudah

20. **Kore**
This

Ini

21. **Sore**
That

Itu

22. **Are**
That thing over there.

Benda di situ.

23. **Kono**
This

Ini

24. **Sono**
That

Itu

25. **Ano**
That one over there.

Yang di sana itu.

26. **Kono hito**
This person

Orang ini

27. **Sono hito**
That person

Orang itu

28. **Ano hito**
That person over there.

Orang yang di sana itu.

29. **Hon**
Book

Buku

30. **Nōto**
Notebook

Buku Catitan

31. **Kami**
Paper

Kertas

32. **Shinbun**
Newspaper

Suratkhabar

33. **Jidōsha, Kuruma**
Car

Kereta

34. **Jitensha**
Bicycle

Basikal

35. **Pen**
Pen

Pena

36. **Bōrupen**
Ball-point pen

Pena mata bulat

37. **Enpitsu**
Pencil

Pensel

38. **Desu**
Is, are

Ialah, adalah

39. **Ja arimasen**
Not

Tidak

40. **Honto**
True

Benar

41. **Omedetō**
Congratulations

Tahniah

42. **Onaji**
Same

Sama

43. **Chigaimasu**
It is wrong.

Ia adalah salah.

44. **Mada**
Not yet

Belum lagi

45. **Sensei**
Teacher

Guru

46. **Gakusei**
Student

Pelajar

47. **Ima**
Now

Kini

48. **Hima**
Free (time)

Masa lapang

49. **Isogashii**
Busy

Sibuk

50. **Tanjōbi**
Birthday

Hari jadi

51. **Bunpō**
Grammar

Nahu

52. **Mondai**
Exercise

Latihan

53. **Dai ... ka**
Lesson ...

Pelajaran ...

54. **Marēishia**
Malaysia

Malaysia

55. **Chūgoku** China	*China*
56. **Firipin** Philippines	*Filipina*
57. **Indo** India	*India*
58. **Indoneshia** ·Indonesia	*Indonesia*
59. **Kankoku** Korea	*Korea*
60. **Nihon** Japan	*Jepun*
61. **Ōsutoraria** Australia	*Australia*
62. **Tai** Thailand	*Negeri Thai*
63. **... jin** person	*Orang*
64. **Marēishia jin** Malaysian	*Orang (rakyat) Malaysia*
65. **...go** ...Language	*Bahasa*
66. **Nihon go** Japanese language	*Bahasa Jepun*

Daisanka – Nichijō Kaiwa
Pelajaran 3 – Perbualan Harian
Lesson 3 – Daily Conversation

1. **Hontō desu ka?**
   Is it true?

   Adakah ia benar?

2. **Wakarimasu ka?**
   Do you understand?

   Adakah anda faham?

3. **Shīteimasu.**
   I know.

   Saya tahu.

4. **Shirimasen.**
   I don't know.

   Saya tidak tahu.

5. **Anata wa doko ni sundeimasu ka?**
   Where do you live?

   Di mana anda tinggal?

6. **Anata no uchi wa doko ni arimasu ka?**
   Where is your house?

   Di manakah rumah anda?

7. **Anata wa doko de hatarakimasu ka?**
   Where do you work?

   Di manakah anda bekerja?

8. **Anata no kaisha wa doko ni arimasu ka?**
   Where is your company?

   Di manakah syarikat anda?

9. **(Anata wa) kekon shimashita ka?**
   Are you married?

   Sudahkah anda berkahwin?

10. **Hai, kekkon shimashita.**
    Yes, I am married.

    Ya, saya sudah berkahwin.

11. **Iie, dokushin desu.**
    No, I am single.

    Tidak, saya masih bujang.

12. **Konyaku shimashita ka?**
    Are you engaged?

    Sudahkah anda bertunang?

13. **Okusan wa hatarakimasu ka?**
    Does your wife work?

    Adakah isteri anda bekerja?

14. **Okusan wa Nihon jin desu ka?**
    Is your wife a Japanese?

    Adakah isteri anda seorang Jepun?

15. **Kochira wa watashi no shujin desu.**
    This is my husband.

    Ini suami saya.

16. **Konokata wa watashi no tomodachi desu.**
    This person is my friend.

    Orang ini sahabat saya.

17. **Sumimasen.**
    Gomen nasai.
    Excuse me.
    I am sorry.

    Maafkan saya.

18. **Shitsurei shimashita.**
    Excuse me (for what is done).

    Maafkan saya (ke atas apa yang telah berlaku).

19. **Kyō wa atsui desu.**
    It is hot today.

    Hari ini panas.

20. **Kyō wa atsui desu ne?**
    It is hot today, isn't it?

    Hari ini panas, bukan?

21. **Kyō wa ii tenki desu.**
    The weather is good today.

    Hari ini cuaca baik.

22. **Kyō wa otenki desu ne?**
    The weather is bad today, isn't
    it?

    Cuaca buruk hari ini, bukan?

23. **Kyō wa hare desu.**
    It is fine (weather) today.

    Cuaca baik pada hari ini.

24. **Kinō wa samui deshita ka?**
    Was yesterday cold?

    Adakah semalam sejuk?

25. **Iie, kinō wa samui ja**
    arimasen deshita.
    No, yesterday was not cold.

    Tidak, semalam tidak sejuk.

26. **Ame ga futeimasu.**
    It is raining.

    Hari sedang hujan.

27. **Ame furi desu.**
    Rainy.

    Berhujan.

28. **Yuki ga furimasu.**
    It is snowing.

    Bersalji.

29. **Kaze ga fukimasu.**
    The wind blows.

    Angin bertiup.

30. **Kaze fuki desu.**
    It is windy.

    Berangin.

Bunpō
Grammar

Tatabahasa

1. (i) **"Deshita"**
         Past Tense of "Desu".
         It means "was" and
         "were"

         Kata lampau bagi "Desu".
         Ini bermaksud, "telah".

Kinō wa samui deshita.
It **was** cold yesterday.

Semalam sejuk.

**Watashi wa sensei
deshita.**
I **was** a teacher.

Saya pernah jadi guru.

(ii) **"Ja (dewa) arimasen
deshita"**
Past Negative of "Desu".
It means "was not" and
"were not".

*Kata lampau negatif bagi
"Desu".
Ini bermakna, "bukan".*

**Watashi wa sensei dewa
arimasen deshita.**
I **was not** a teacher.

Saya bukan seorang guru.

**Watashi tachi wa gakusei
ja arimasen deshita.**
We **were not** students.

Kami bukan murid.

2. **"Wa", "Ga"**
"Wa" and "Ga" have no
equivalent in Bahasa Malaysia
or even in English. They
usually come before the subject
or topic in a sentence.

*"Wa" dan "Ga" tiada
persamaannya dalam Bahasa
Malaysia atau Bahasa Inggeris.
Ia selalunya digunakan di
hadapan perkara atau topik
dalam ayat.*

Distinction between "Wa" and
"Ga".
(i) **Watashi wa Taro desu.**
I am Taro.

*Perbezaan antara "Wa" dan
"Ga".
Saya ialah Taro.*

In the above sentence "wa"
emphasizes **Mr. Taro** and
not "I".

*Dalam ayat di atas "wa"
menegaskan "En. Taro" dan
bukan "Saya".*

(ii) **Watashi ga Taro desu.**
I am Taro.

Saya ialah Taro.

In this sentence "ga" emphasizes "I" and not "Mr. Taro".

Dalam ayat ini "ga" menegaskan "Saya" dan bukan "En. Taro".

3. **"Ne"**
Means "isn't it".

"Ne" bermakna "bukankah".

  (i) **Atsui desu ne?**
It is hot, **isn't it?**

Ia panas, bukan?

  (ii) **Kirei desu ne?**
It is beautiful, **isn't it?**

Ia cantik, bukan?

4. **"De"**
  (a) denotes a place and means "at".

"De" menandakan tempat dan "di".

    (i) **Watashi wa Matsushita de hatarakimasu.**
I work **at** Matsushita.

Saya bekerja di Matsushita.

    (ii) **Watashi tachi wa UMW de hatarakimasu.**
We work at UMW.

Kami bekerja di UMW.

  (b) "De" also means "with" and "by".

"De" juga bermakna "dengan" dan "melalui".

    (i) **Takushii de ikimashita.**
I went **by** taxi.

Saya pergi dengan teksi.

    (ii) **Mimi de nani o shimasu ka?**
What do you do with (your) ears?

Apa anda buat dengan telinga anda?

(iii) **Mimi de oto o kikimasu.** *Saya dengar bunyi dengan telinga saya.*
I hear sounds with my ears.

5. Dōshi — *Katakerja*
Verbs

Kata sekarang Present Tense ... masu	Bentuk kamus Dictionary Form ... u	Kata lampau Past Tense ... mashita	Erti katakerja (Kata sekarang)
hairimasu enter	hairu	hairimashita entered	masuk
suwarimasu sit	suwaru	suwarimashita sat	duduk
wakarimasu understand	wakaru	wakarimashita understood	faham
shirimasu know	shiru	shirimashita knew	tahu
hatarakimasu work	hataraku	hatarakimashita worked	kerja
kekkon shimasu marry	kekkon suru	kekkon shimashita married	kahwin
konyaku shimasu to get engaged	konyaku suru	konyaku shimashita engaged	bertunang
ikimasu go	iku	ikimashita went	pergi
kikimasu hear, listen	kiku	kikimashita heard, listened	dengar
sumimasu live	sumu	sumimashita lived	hidup

A. Mijikai Kaiwa.
A Short Conversation.
Satu Perbualan Rengkas.

A: **Anata wa Marēishia jin desu ka?**
B: **Hai, ---**

A: **Doko ni sundeimasu ka?**
B: **---**

A: **Doko de hatarakimasu ka?**
B: **---**

A: **Kyō wa atsui desu ne?**
B: **Hai, ---**
   Iie, ---

A: **Kinō wa samui deshita ka?**
B: **Hai, kino wa ---**
   Iie, ---

A: **Kekkon shimashita ka?**
B: **Hai, ---**
   Iie, ---

B. *Tukarkan ayat-ayat berikut ke dalam kata lampau.*
Change these sentences into the past tense.

1. **Kore wa bōrupen desu.**

2. **Ano hito wa sensei desu.**

3. **Kyō wa isōgashii ja arimasen.**

4. **Kanojo wa hima desu.**

5. **Kyō wa atsui ja arimasen.**

6. Marēishia jin wa kirei desu.

7. Kare wa Taro san ja arimasen.

8. Donata wa Taro san desu ka?

9. Anata no kaisha wa doko desu ka?

10. Kore wa donata no enpitsu desu ka?

11. Anata wa doko de hatarakimasu ka?

12. Wakarimasu ka?

13. Itsu kekkon shimasuka?

14. Doko ni sumimasu ka?

C. *Susun semula ayat-ayat berikut dengan betul.*
Rearrange the following sentences correctly.

1. doko hatarakimasu de ka wa anata.

2. Taro san kono kata desu wa.

3. ja arimasen wa sensei watashi tomodachi no.

4. Nihon jin wa kare ka desu.

5. ikimashita naze Tōkyō ka ni.

6. kekkon ka shimashita itsu.

7. jidōsha wa de watashi ikimashita.

8. genki dōmo arigatō desu hai.

Hombun	*Perbendaharaan Kata*
Glossary	

1. **Honto**
   True
   Benar

2. **Wakarimasu**
   Understand
   Faham

3. **Shirimasu**
   Know
   Tahu

4. **Sumimasu**
   Live
   Tinggal

5. **Hatarakimasu**
   Work
   Bekerja

6. **Kekkon**
   Marriage
   Perkahwinan

7. **Kekkon shimasu**
   Marry
   Kahwin

8. **Dokushin**
   Single
   Bujang

9. **Konyaku shimasu**
   To get engaged
   Bertunang

10. **Kodomo**
    Child
    Budak

11. **Kodomo tachi**
    Children
    Kanak-kanak

12. **Kochira**
    This
    Ini

13. **Konó kata**   *Orang ini*
    This person

14. **Tomodachi**   *Sahabat*
    Friend

15. **Sumimasen, Gomen nasai**   *Maafkan saya*
    Excuse me

16. **Atsui**   *Panas*
    Hot

17. **Samui**   *Sejuk*
    Cold

18. **Suzushi**   *Dingin*
    Cool

19. **Atatakai**   *Hangat*
    Warm

20. **Ame**   *Hujan*
    Rain

21. **Yuki**   *Salji*
    Snow

22. **Kaze**   *Angin*
    Wind

23. **Furimasu**   *Turun (hujan)*
    Falls (e.g. for rain, snow etc.)

24. **Fukimasu**   *Tiup (angin)*
    Blows (e.g. for wind)

25. **Kyō**   *Hari ini*
    Today

26. **Kinō**
    Yesterday

    Semalam

27. **Ano kata, Ano hito**
    That person over there.

    Orang yang di sana itu.

28. **Ryōshin**
    Parents

    Ibubapa

29. **Fūfu**
    Married couple.

    Pasangan yang telah berkahwin.

30. **Otōsan**
    (i) Your father.
    (ii) Someone's father.

    (i) Bapa awak.
    (ii) Bapa seseorang.

31. **Chichi**
    My father.

    Bapa saya.

32. **Okāsan**
    (i) Your mother.
    (ii) Someone's mother.

    (i) Ibu anda.
    (ii) Ibu seseorang.

33. **Haha**
    My mother.

    Ibu saya.

34. **Ojiisan**
    (i) Your grandfather.
    (ii) Someone's grandfather.

    (i) Datuk anda.
    (ii) Datuk seseorang.

35. **Sofu**
    My grandfather.

    Datuk saya.

36. **Obāsan**
    (i) Your grandmother.
    (ii) Someone's grandmother.

    (i) Nenek anda.
    (ii) Nenek seseorang.

37. **Sobo**
    My grandmother.

    Nenek saya.

38. **Go shujin**
    (i) Your husband.
    (ii) Someone's husband.

    (i) Suami kamu.
    (ii) Suami seseorang.

39. **Shujin**
    My husband.

    Suami saya.

40. **Okusan**
    (i) Your wife.
    (ii) Someone's wife.

    (i) Isteri anda.
    (ii) Isteri seseorang.

41. **Tsuma, Kanai**
    My wife.

    Isteri saya.

42. **Bochan**
    (i) Your son.
    (ii) Someone's son.

    (i) Anak lelaki anda.
    (ii) Anak lelaki seseorang.

43. **Ojōsan**
    (i) Your daughter.
    (ii) Someone's daughter.

    (i) Anak perempuan anda.
    (ii) Anak perempuan seseorang.

44. **Musume**
    Daughter.

    Anak perempuan saya.

45. **Oniisan**
    (i) Your elder brother.
    (ii) Someone's elder brother.

    (i) Abang anda.
    (ii) Abang seseorang.

46. **Ani**
    My elder brother.

    Abang saya.

47. **Onēsan**
    (i) Your elder sister.
    (ii) Someone's elder sister.

    (i) Kakak anda.
    (ii) Kakak seseorang.

48. **Ane**
My elder sister.

Kakak saya.

49. **Otōtosan**
  (i) Your younger brother.
  (ii) Someone's younger brother.

  (i) Adik anda.
  (ii) Adik seseorang.

50. **Otōto**
My younger brother.

Adik lelaki saya.

51. **Imōtosan**
  (i) Your younger sister.
  (ii) Someone's younger sister.

  (i) Adik perempuan anda.
  (ii) Adik perempuan seseorang.

52. **Imōto**
My younger sister.

Adik perempuan saya.

53. **Kyōdai**
Brothers

Adik-beradik lelaki.

54. **Shimai**
Sisters

Adik-beradik perempuan.

55. **Itoko**
Cousin

Sepupu

56. **Mei**
Niece

Anak saudara perempuan.

57. **Oi**
Nephew

Anak saudara lelaki.

58. **Ichiban**
Most, best

Paling baik.

59. **Chōnan**
Eldest son.

Anak lelaki sulung.

60. **Chōjo**
    Eldest daughter.

Anak perempuan sulung.

61. **Atama**
    Head

Kepala

62. **I, Onaka**
    Stomach

Perut

63. **Me**
    Eyes

Mata

64. **Hana**
    Nose

Hidung

65. **Mimi**
    Ears

Telinga

66. **Kuchi**
    Mouth

Mulut

67. **Nodo**
    Throat

Kerongkong

68. **Kubi**
    Neck

Tengkok

69. **Te**
    Hand

Tangan

70. **Ashi**
    Legs

Kaki

71. **Ude**
    Arm

Lengan

72. **Yubi**
    Finger

Jari

73. **Kakato**   *Buku lali*
    Ankle

74. **Mune**   *Dada*
    Chest

75. **Hai**   *Paru-paru*
    Lung

76. **Chō**   *Usus*
    Intestines

77. **Mōchōen**   *Appendictis*
    Appendicitis

78. **Shinzō**   *Jantung*
    Heart

79. **Bōkō**   *Gelembong*
    Bladder

Daiyonka - Kyoshitsu de
Pelajaran 4 - Dibilik Darjah
Lesson 4 - In the Classroom

1. **Watashi wa sensei desu.**
   I am a teacher.

   Saya seorang guru.

2. **Watashi wa Nihongo o**
   ōshiemasu.
   I teach the Japanese language.

   Saya mengajar Bahasa Jepun.

3. **Donata san wa Nihongo o**
   benkyō shimasu ka?
   Who studies the Japanese
   language?

   Siapa yang belajar Bahasa
   Jepun?

4. **Watashi tachi wa Nihongo o**
   benkyō shimasu.
   We study the Japanese
   language.

   Kami belajar Bahasa Jepun.

5. **Watashi tachi wa Nihongo o**
   benkyō shimasen.
   We do not (don't) study the
   Japanese language.

   Kami tidak belajar Bahasa
   Jepun.

6. **Anata wa Nihongo o**
   wakarimasu ka?
   Do you understand the
   Japanese language?

   Anda faham Bahasa Jepun?

   Hai, chotto wakarimasu.
   Yes, I understand a little..

   Ya, saya faham sedikit.

   Hai, yoku wakarimasu.
   Yes, I understand well.

   Ya, saya faham dengan baik.

   Iie, wakarimasen.
   No, I don't understand.

   Tidak, saya tidak faham.

7. **Mō ichido oshatte kudasai.** *Tolong ulang sekali lagi.*
   Please say it once more.

8. **Issho ni yonde kudasai.** *Tolong bacakan bersama.*
   Please read it together.

9. **Issho ni mite kudasai.** *Tolong lihat bersama.*
   Please see it together.

10. **Issho ni kiite kudasai.** *Tolong dengar bersama.*
    Please listen together.

11. **Issho ni kaite kudasai.** *Tolong tulis bersama.*
    Please write together.

12. **Mō ichido kaite kudasai.** *Tolong tulis sekali lagi.*
    Please write it once more.

13. **Kurikaeshite kudasai.** *Tolong ulang.*
    Please repeat.

14. **Yoku dekimashita.** *Anda telah buat dengan baik.*
    (You) did well.

15. **Shitsumon shite kudasai.** *Tolong tanya soalan.*
    Please ask questions.

16. **Kotaete kudasai.** *Tolong jawap.*
    Please answer.

17. **Motto ōkina koe de itte** *Tolong cakap dengan kuat.*
    kudasai.
    Please say it louder.

18. **Isoide kudasai.** *Tolong cepat.*
    Hurry up, please.

19. **Yukkuri hanashite kudasai.** *Tolong cakap perlahan-lahan.*
    Please speak slowly.

20. **Mata ashita.**
    See you again, tomorrow.

Jumpa lagi, esok.

I. **Bunpō**
   Grammar

Tatabahasa

"O" denotes object in a
sentence.

*"O" menandakan objek dalam
satu ayat.*

1. **Hon o yomimasu.**
   I read a book.
2. **Nihongo o benkyō shimasu.**
   I study the Japanese language.

Saya membaca sebuah buku.

Saya belajar Bahasa Jepun.

II. **Dōshi**
    Verbs

Perbuatan

Kata sekarang	Bentuk kamus	Kata sekarang (negatif)	Bentuk suruhan (halus)	Erti katakerja (kata sekarang)
Present Tense	Dictionary Form	Present Negative	Please Form	
...masu	...u	...masen	...te kudasai ...de kudasai	
oshiemasu	oshieru	oshiemasen	oshiete kudasai	*mengajar*
teach		will not teach does not teach	please teach	
benkyō shimasu	benkyō suru	benkyō shimasen	benkyō shite kudasai	*belajar*
study		will not study does not study	please study	
wakarimasu	wakaru	wakarimasen	wakate kudasai	*faham*
understand		don't understand	please understand	

mimasu see	miru	mimasen will not see does not see	mite kudasai please see	*lihat*
kikimasu listen	kiku	kikimasen will not listen does not listen	kiite kudasai please listen	*dengar*
dekimasu can	dekiru	dekimasen cannot	dekite kudasai	*boleh*
isogimasu hurry	isogu	isogimasen will not hurry does not hurry	isoide kudasai please hurry	*lekas*
hanashimasu speak	hanasu	hanashimasen will not speak does not speak	hanshite kudasai please speak	*cakap*
kurikaeshi- masu repeat	kurikaesu	kurikaeshi- masen will not repeat does not repeat	kurikaeshite kudasai please repeat	*ulang*
kakimasu write	kaku	kakimasen will not write does not write	kaite kudasai please write	*tulis*

A. Translate the following conversation into Japanese.

Terjemahkan perbualan berikut ke dalam Bahasa Jepun.

A: Are you a Japanese?

B: No, I am not a Japanese. I am a Malaysian.

A: Adakah anda orang Jepun?

B: Tidak, saya bukan orang Jepun. Saya orang Malaysia.

A: Do you speak Japanese?	A: Bolehkah anda bercakap Bahasa Jepun?
B: Yes, I speak a little.	B: Ya, saya boleh bercakap sedikit.

A: Please write your name.	A: Tolong tulis nama anda.
B: This is my name. Please read it.	B: Ini nama saya. Tolong bacakannya.

A: Who is your Japanese language teacher?	A: Siapakah guru Bahasa Jepun anda?
B: He is Mr. Kato.	B: Beliau ialah Encik Kato.

A: Please say it once more.	A: Tolong ulang sekali lagi.
B: He is Mr. Kato. Do you know him?	B: Beliau ialah Encik Kato. Anda kenal diakah?

A: No, I do not know him.	A: Tidak, saya tidak kenal beliau.
B: He is over there. Please meet him. B to Mr. Kato: This person is Mr. A.	B: Dia di sana. Tolong jumpa dia. B kepada Encik Kato: Orang ini ialah Encik A.

A: I am A. Glad to meet you.	A: Saya A. Saya gembira bertemu dengan anda.

Kato: How do you do? Please sit down.	Kato: Apa khabar? Sila duduk.

B: Thank you.	B: Terima kasih.

B. What would you say? *Apa yang anda akan kata?*

1. When you are late. *Bila anda terlambat.*

2. When you ask someone to *Bila anda meminta seseorang*

repeat what he has just said (i.e. I beg your pardon).	*mengulang apa yang baru dikatakannya (contoh saya minta maaf, boleh ulang).*
3. When you ask someone to enter.	*Apabila anda minta seseorang supaya masuk.*
4. When you ask someone to sit.	*Apabila anda minta seseorang supaya duduk.*
5. When you introduce yourself.	*Apabila anda memperkenalkan diri.*
6. When you understand a little (a bit).	*Apabila anda faham sedikit.*
7. When you ask someone to answer (a question).	*Apabila anda minta seseorang untuk menjawab (satu soalan).*
8. When you ask someone to say it louder.	*Apabila anda minta seseorang mengatakannya dengan kuat.*
9. When you ask someone whether he/she understands Japanese.	*Apabila anda minta seseorang sama ada dia memahami Bahasa Jepun.*
10. When you wish someone (i) Happy New Year. (ii) Good evening. (iii) Good night.	*Apabila anda mengucapkan kepada seseorang (i) Selamat Tahun Baru. (ii) Selamat petang. (iii) Selamat malam.*

C.

Isikan tempat-tempat kosong.
Fill in the blanks.

Kata sekarang Present Tense	Bentuk kamus Dictionary Form	Kata sekarang (negatif) Present Negative	Bentuk suruhan (halus) Please Form
kotaemasu			
	hairu		
	iku		
			hataraite kudasai
		yomimasen	
		hanashimasen	
mimasu			
	kekkon suru		
		kakimasen	
shitsumon shimasu			

Hombun
Glossary

Perbendaharaan kata

1. **Hajimemasu**
   Begin

   Mula

2. **Yomimasu**
   Read

   Baca

3. **Mimasu**
   See

   Lihat

4. **Benkyō shimasu**
   Study

   Belajar

5. **Iimasu**
   Say

   Berkata

6. **Oshiemasu**   *Mengajar*
   Teach

7. **Naraimasu**   *Belajar*
   Learn

8. **Kotae**   *Jawab (katanama)*
   Answer (noun)

9. **Kotaemasu**   *Menjawab (perbuatan)*
   To answer (verb)

10. **Shitsumon**   *Soalan (katanama)*
    Question (noun)

11. **Shitsumon shimasu**   *Menyoal*
    To question (verb)

12. **Hanashimasu**   *Cakap*
    Speak

13. **Ōkii**   *Besar*
    Big

14. **Chiisai**   *Kecil*
    Small

15. **Muzukashii**   *Susah*
    Difficult

16. **Kantan, Yasashi**   *Mudah*
    Easy

17. **Jōzu**   *Bijak*
    Clever

18. **Heta**   *Tidak mahir*
    Not skilled

19. **Bunpō** Grammar

Tatabahasa

20. **Bun** Sentence

Ayat

21. **Tango** Single words

Perkataan tunggal

22. **Boin** Vowel

Vokal

23. **Shiin** Consonant

Konsonan

24. **Renshū** Practice

Amalan

25. **Meishi** Noun

Katanama

26. **Keiyōshi** Adjective

Adjektif

27. **Fukushi** Adverb

Adverba

28. **Sūji** Numerals

Angka

29. **Genzai** Present

Sekarang

30. **Kako** Past

Lampau

31. **Fukushū** Review

Meninjau kembali

32. **Rei** *Contoh*
    Example

33. **Honyaku** *Terjemahan*
    Translation

34. **Honyaku shimasu** *Terjemahkan*
    Translate

Daigoka – Kazu, Toki
Pelajaran 5 – Nombor, Masa
Lesson 5 – Number, Time

1. **Anata wa nan sai desu ka?**
   Anata wa ikutsu desu ka?
   How old are you?

   Berapakah umur anda?

2. **Watashi wa nijū-san sai desu.**
   I am 23 years old.

   Umur saya 23 tahun.

3. **Hon ga ikutsu arimasu ka?**
   How many books do you have?

   Berapa banyakkah buku yang anda miliki?

4. **Hon ga jū-ichi arimasu.**
   I have 11 books.

   Saya mempunyai 11 buah buku.

5. **Hon ga arimasen deshita.**
   I did not have any books.

   Saya tidak mempunyai buku.

6. **Kono hon wa ikura desu ka?**
   How much is this book?

   Berapakah harga buku ini?

7. **Kono hon wa 3,000 (san sen) en desu.**
   This book is 3,000 yen.

   Buku ini berharga 3,000 yen.

8. **Anata wa ikura arimasu ka?**
   How much money do you have?

   Berapa banyakkah wang yang anda ada?

9. **Watashi wa 1,500 (sen gohyaku) en ga arimasu.**
   I have 1,500 yen.

   Saya ada 1,500 yen.

10. **Ichibanme no hito wa koko ni kite kudasai.**
The first person, come here please.

Orang pertama diharap datang ke sini.

11. **Watashi no uchi (ie) wa kono uchi no sanbai desu.**
My house is (three times) larger than this house.

Rumah saya (tiga kali) lebih besar daripada rumah ini.

12. **Watashi no heya wa kono heya no sambun no ichi desu.**
My room is ⅓ (one-third) the size of this room.

Luas bilik saya satu pertiga luas bilik ini.

13. **Kore wa tokei desu.**
This is a clock.

Ini sebuah jam.

14. **Ima nanji desu ka?**
What time is it now?

Pukul berapakah sekarang?

15. **3 (san) ji desu.**
It is three o'clock.

Sekarang pukul tiga.

16. **Chōdo 3 (san) ji desu.**
It is exactly three o'clock.

Sekarang tepat pukul tiga.

17. **3 (san) ji jūpun mae desu.**
10 minutes to three.

Sepuluh minit lagi pukul tiga.

18. **3 (san) ji jūpun sugi desu.**
10 minutes past three.

Pukul tiga sepuluh minit.

19. **Watashi no tokei wa atteimasu (tadashii desu).**
My watch is correct.

Jam saya tepat.

20. **Anata no tokei wa okuriteimasu.**
Your watch is slow.

Jam anda lambat.

21. **Kare no tokei wa susundeimasu.**
His watch is fast.

Jam dia cepat.

22. **Kinō wa hatarakimashita ka?**
Did you work yesterday?

Adakah anda bekerja semalam?

23. **Hai, hatarakimashita.**
Yes, I worked (yesterday).

Ya, saya bekerja (semalam).

24. **Iie, hatarakimasen deshita.**
No, I did not work (yesterday).

Tidak, saya tidak bekerja (semalam).

25. **Nanji kara hatarakimasu ka?**
What time do you start work?

Pukul berapakah anda mulai bekerja?

26. **Nanji kara nanji made hatarakimashita ka?**
From what time to what time did you work?

Dari pukul berapa hingga pukul berapakah anda telah bekerja?

27. **Gozen 8 (hachi) ji kara gogo 5 (go) ji made hatarakimashita.**
I worked from 8 a.m. to 5 p.m.

Saya telah bekerja dari pukul 8.00 pagi hingga 5.00 petang.

28. **Gozen 6 (roko) ji ni hatarakimasu ka?**
Do you work at 6 a.m.?

Adakah anda bekerja pada pukul 6.00 pagi?

29. **Hai, hatarakimasu.**
Yes, I work (at 6 a.m.).

Ya, saya bekerja (pada pukul 6.00 pagi).

30. **Kinō no ban (yube) wa 8 (hachi) ji ni nemashita.**
Last night, I slept at 8 p.m.

Malam tadi, saya tidur pukul 8.00 malam.

31. **Kinō no ban wa nemasen deshita.**
I did not sleep last night.

Saya tidak tidur malam tadi.

32. **Koko kara soko made nanjikan kakarimasu ka?**
How long does it take from here to there?

Berapa lamakah perjalanan dari sini ke sana?

33. **Koko kara soko made I(ichi) jikan kakarimasu.**
It takes 1 hour and 5 minutes (from here to there).

Dari sini ke sana mengambil masa satu jam lima minit.

34. **Nihongo no jūgyo wa nanjikan desu ka?**
How long is the Japanese class?

Berapa lamakah kelas Bahasa Jepun?

35. **I (ichi) jikan 30 (sanjjū) pun desu.**
It is 1 hour 30 minutes.

Satu jam 30 minit.

Ichinichi wa nijū yojikan desu.
One day has 24 hours.

Sehari 24 jam.

36. **Hiruma wa asa kara yūgata made desu.**
Daytime (Daylight) is from morning to evening.

Waktu siang dari pagi hingga petang.

37. **Yoru wa yūgata kara asa made desu.**
Night (Night-time) is from evening to (until) morning.

Waktu malam dari petang hingga (sampai) pagi.

I. **Bunpō**
Grammar

Tatabahasa

  (a) "Ni"
    "Ni" denotes time and means "at".
      (i) **(Watashi wa) 3 (san) ji ni benkyō shimashita.**
      I studied at 3 o'clock.

"Ni" menandakan masa dan bererti "pada"
Saya telah belajar pada pukul tiga.

(ii) **(Watashi wa) 3 (san) ji ni benkyō shimasen deshita.**
I did not study at 3 o'clock.

Saya tidak belajar pada pukul tiga.

(b) "Ni" also denotes purpose and means "for".
  (i) **Kaimono ni ikimasen deshita.**
  I did not go shopping.
  (ii) **Kono hon wa anata ni okurimasen deshita.**
  I did not send this book for you.

"Ni" juga menandakan tujuan dan bererti "untuk".
Saya tidak pergi membeli-belah.

Saya tidak menghantar buku ini untuk anda.

(c) "Ni" also denotes the direction and means "to". "Ni" is also similar to "e".
Watashi wa Tōkyō ni(e) ikimashita.
I went to Tokyo.

"Ni" juga menandakan arah dan bererti "kepada". "Ni" juga mempunyai persamaan dengan "e" saya pergi ke Tokyo.
Saya telah pergi ke Tokyo.

(d) "Ni" also denotes place. In this sense it means "in".
  (i) **Watashi to Kare ga Tōkyō ni sundeimasu.**
  I and he live in Tokyo.

"Ni" juga menandakan tempat. Dalam hal ini bererti "di".
Saya dan dia tinggal di Tokyo.

II. Doshi
Verbs

Perbuatan

Kata sekarang / Present Tense / ... masu	Bentuk kamus / Dictionary Form / ... u	Kata lampau (negatif) / Past Negative / ... masen deshita	Erti katakerja (Kata sekarang)
arimasu have	aru	arimasen deshita did not have	ada

kimasu come	kuru	kimasen deshita did not come	*datang*
nemasu sleep	neru	nemasen deshita did not sleep	*tidur*
okimasu get up, wake up	okiru	okimasen deshita did not get up, did not wake up	*bangun*
kakarimasu takes (time)	kakaru	kakarimasen deshita did not take (time)	*ambil (masa)*
tsukarimasu tired	tsukareru	tsukarimasen deshita was not tired	*penat*
kaerimasu return	kaeru	kaerimasen deshita did not return	*pulang*
kazoemasu count	kazoeru	kazoemasen deshita did not count	*kira*
tabemasu eat	taberu	tabemasen deshita did not eat	*makan*
nomimasu drink	nomu	nomimasen deshita did not drink	*minum*

A. Translate the following sentences into Japanese.

Terjemahkan ayat-ayat berikut ke dalam Bahasa Jepun.

A. What is the time now?

Pukul berapakah sekarang?

B. It is 3 o'clock.

Sekarang pukul tiga.

A. Is your watch (time) correct?

Adakah jam anda tepat?

B. Yes, it is so.

Ya, begitulah.

| A. | No, your watch (time) is fast. | *Tidak, jam anda cepat.* |
| B. | Is it so? | *Benarkah begitu?* |

| A. | Yes, it is so. | *Ya, memang benar.* |
| B. | How many minutes fast is it? | *Berapa minitkah cepatnya?* |

| A. | (By) Ten minutes. | *Sepuluh minit.* |

B. Translate the following sentences into Japanese. — *Terjemahkan ayat-ayat berikut ke dalam Bahasa Jepun.*

1. Are there 24 hours in a day? — *Adakah sehari 24 jam?*

2. I did not get up. — *Saya tidak bangun.*

3. How many minutes are there in one hour? — *Berapa minitkah dalam sejam?*

4. How many hours does it take from C to D by bus? — *Berapa jamkah masa perjalanan dari C ke D dengan bas?*

5. It takes 5 hours. — *Lamanya 5 jam.*

6. He did not eat until 3 p.m. — *Dia tidak makan sehingga pukul tiga petang.*

7. The first person will sit here, please. — *Orang pertama silalah duduk di sini.*

8. This company is one quarter the size (of) your company. — *Syarikat ini sebesar satu per empat syarikat anda.*

C. *Isikan tempat-tempat kosong.*
Fill in the blanks.

Bentuk kamus Dictionary Form	*Kata lampau negatif* Past Negative
hairu	
suwaru	
shiru	
oshieru	
benkyō suru	
wakaru	
aru	
kuru	
neru	
kazoeru	
tsukareru	
kaeru	

Hombun
 Glossary

Perbendaharaan kata

1. **Ichi**
 One

   Satu

2. **Ni**
 Two

   Dua

3. **San**
 Three

   Tiga

4. **Shi, Yon**   *Empat*
   Four

5. **Go**   *Lima*
   Five

6. **Roku**   *Enam*
   Six

7. **Shichi, Nana** *Tujuh*
   Seven

8. **Hachi**   *Lapan*
   Eight

9. **Ku, Kyū**   *Sembilan*
   Nine

10. **Jū**   *Sepuluh*
    Ten

11. **Jūichi**   *Sebelas*
    Eleven

12. **Jūni**   *Dua belas*
    Twelve

13. **Jūsan**   *Tiga belas*
    Thirteen

14. **Jūyon, Jūshi** *Empat belas*
    Fourteen

15. **Jūgo**   *Lima belas*
    Fifteen

16. **Jūroku**   *Enam belas*
    Sixteen

17. **Jūnana, Jūshichi** *Tujuh belas*
    Seventeen

18. **Jūhachi**
    Eighteen

    Lapan belas

19. **Jūku, Jūkyū**
    Nineteen

    Sembilan belas

20. **Nijū**
    Twenty

    Dua puluh

21. **Nijūichi**
    Twenty-one

    Dua puluh satu

22. **Nijūni**
    Twenty-two

    Dua puluh dua

23. **Sanjū**
    Thirty

    Tiga puluh

24. **Yonjū**
    Forty

    Empat puluh

25. **Gojū**
    Fifty

    Lima puluh

26. **Rokujū**
    Sixty

    Enam puluh

27. **Nanajū**
    Seventy

    Tujuh puluh

28. **Hachijū**
    Eighty

    Lapan puluh

29. **Kujū, Kyūjū**
    Ninety

    Sembilan puluh

30. **Hyaku**
    One hundred

    Seratus

31. **Sen**
    One thousand

    Seribu

32. **Man** *Sepuluh ribu*
   Ten thousand

33. **Jūman** *Seratus ribu*
   One hundred thousand

34. **Hyakuman** *Sejuta*
   One million

35. **Senman** *Sepuluh juta*
   Ten million

36. **Oku** *Seratus juta*
   One hundred million

37. **Jūoku** *Satu billion*
   One billion

38. **Hyakuoku** *Sepuluh billion*
   Ten billion

39. **Senoku** *Seratus billion*
   Hundred billion

40. **- Ji -** *Pukul*
   - o'clock -

   Ichiji *Pukul satu*
   One o'clock

   Niji *Pukul dua*
   Two o'clock

   Sanji *Pukul tiga*
   Three o'clock

   Yoji *Pukul empat*
   Four o'clock

   Goji *Pukul lima*
   Five o'clock

Rokuji
Six o'clock

Pukul enam

Shichiji, Nanaji
Seven o'clock

Pukul tujuh

Hachiji
Eight o'clock

Pukul lapan

Kuji
Nine o'clock

Pukul sembilan

Jūji
Ten o'clock

Pukul sepuluh

Jūichiji
Eleven o'clock

Pukul sebelas

Jūniji
Twelve o'clock

Pukul dua belas

Nanji desu ka?
What is the time now?

Pukul berapakah sekarang?

41. **- Fun -**
    - Minute -

Minit

Ippun
One minute

Satu minit

Nifun
Two minutes

Dua minit

Sampun
Three minutes

Tiga minit

Yompun
Four minutes

Empat minit

Gofun
Five minutes

Lima minit

Roppun Six minutes	*Enam minit*
Shichifun, Nanafun Seven minutes	*Tujuh minit*
Hachifun, Happun Eight minutes	*Lapan minit*
Kufun, Kyūfun Nine minutes	*Sembilan minit*
Jippun, Jūppun Ten minutes	*Sepuluh minit*
Jūgofun Fifteen minutes	*Lima belas minit*
Sanjūppun Thirty minutes	*Tiga puluh minit*
Nanpun desu ka? How many minutes?	*Berapa minit?*
42. **- Jikan -** - Hour -	*Jam (masa)*
Ichijikan One hour	*Satu jam*
Nijikan Two hours	*Dua jam*
Sanjikan Three hours	*Tiga jam*
Yojikan Four hours	*Empat jam*
Gojikan Five hours	*Lima jam*

Rokujikan Six hours	*Enam jam*
Shichijikan Seven hours	*Tujuh jam*
Hachijikan Eight hours	*Lapan jam*
Kujikan Nine hours	*Sembilan jam*
Jūjikan Ten hours	*Sepuluh jam*
Nanjikan desu ka? How many hours?	*Berapa jam?*

43. **Gogo**
    Afternoon, p.m.   *Petang*

44. **Gozen**
    Forenoon   *Sebelum tengahari*

45. **Asa**
    Morning, a.m.   *Pagi*

46. **Yoru, Ban**
    Night   *Malam*

47. **Yūgata**
    Evening   *Petang*

48. **Hiruma**
    Daytime   *Waktu siang*

49. **Kakarimasu**
    Takes (time)   *Mengambil (masa)*

50. **Tabemasu**
    Eat   *Makan*

51. **Nomimasu** Drink	*Minum*
52. **Kaerimasu** Return	*Pulang*
53. **Kimasu** Come	*Datang*
54. **Kazoemasu** Count	*Kira, Hitung*
55. **Tsukaremasu** Tired	*Letih*
56. **Kara** From	*Dari/daripada*
57. **Made** Until	*Sehingga*
58. **Ikura** How much (price)?	*Berapakah (harga)?*
59. **Tokei** (i) Clock, (ii) Watch	*(i) Jam besar (ii) Jam tangan*
60. **Hari** Needle	*Jarum*
61. **Chōdo** Exactly	*Tepat*
62. **Sugi** Past	*Lepas*
63. **Mae** Before	*Sebelum*
64. **Han** Half	*Separuh*

65. **Attemasu (tadashi)** *Tepat*
  Correct

66. **Susumimasu** *(i) Pantas (masa), (ii) Memaju*
  (i) Fast (time),
  (ii) To progress

67. **Okuremasu** *Perlahan-lahan*
  Slowly

68. **Ichibanme** *Pertama*
  First

69. **Nibanme** *Kedua*
  Second

70. **Hyakubanme** *Keseratus*
  One hundredth

71. **Nibun no ichi (hanbun)** *Separuh*
  Half

72. **Jūbun no ichi** *Satu per sepuluh*
  One-tenth

Dairokka - Sūshi
Pelajaran 6 - Angka
Lesson 6 - The Numerals

In Japanese as in the case of Chinese and Bahasa Malaysia, numeral classifiers are used when counting various objects. The classifiers to be used usually depends on the shape of the objects, e.g. when counting the number of persons, such words as "nin" are used.

Dalam Bahasa Jepun seperti Bahasa China dan Bahasa Malaysia kata bilangan digunakan apabila mengira berbagai objek. Pengklasan ini selalunya bergantung kepada bentuk objek, contohnya apabila mengira jumlah orang perkataan seperti 'nin' digunakan.

1. **Nannin imasu ka?**
   How many people are there?

   Berapa ramaikah orang yang berada di situ?

2. **Hachinin imasu.**
   There are eight people.

   Terdapat lapan orang di situ.

3. **Futari wa onna de, roku nin wa otoko desu.**
   Two are girls and six are boys.

   Dua budak perempuan dan enam budak lelaki.

4. **Onna no ko wa nannin (ikunin) imasu ka?**
   How many girls are there?

   Berapa ramaikah budak perempuan di situ?

5. **Hitori, futari, sannin, yonin, gonin, rokunin ...**
   One, two, three, four, five, six ...

   Satu, dua, tiga, empat, lima, enam ...

6. **Onna no ko wa zenbu de rokunin imasu.**
   There are altogether six girls.

   Terdapat (jumlahnya) enam budak perempuan di situ.

7. **Kiño wa kaimono ni ikima-shita.**
   Yesterday I went shopping.

   Semalam saya pergi membeli-belah.

8. **Sansatsu hon to, sanzoku kutsu to, yonhon enpitsu to, hachimai kami ga kaimashita.**
   I bought three books, three pairs of shoes, four pencils, and eight sheets of paper.

   Saya membeli 3 buah buku, 3 pasang kasut, 4 batang pensel dan lapan keping kertas.

9. **Issatsu hon wa ikura desu ka?**
   How much is one book?

   Berapakah harga sebuah buku?

10. **1,500 (sen gohyaku) en desu.**
    It costs 1,500 yen.

    Harganya ialah 1,500 yen.

11. **Kono enpitsu wa ippon ikura desu ka?**
    How much is this pencil?

    Berapakah harga sebatang (dari ini) pensel?

12. **Sore wa ippon 50 (gojū) en desu.**
    Each costs 50 yen.

    Sebatang dari ini ialah 50 yen.

13. **Kono kutsu wa isoku 1,000 (sen) en de, sono kutsu wa isoku 2,000 (nisen) desu.**
    Each pair of these socks cost 1,000 yen and a pair of those costs 2,000 yen.

    Sepasang (yang ini) sarung kaki harganya 1,000 yen dan sepa-sang itu ialah 2,000 yen.

14. **Satō wa ichikiroguramu ikura desu ka?**
    How much is 1 kilogram of sugar?

    Berapakah harga 1 kilogram gula?

15. **Ashita wa, mō ichido kaimono ni ikitai desu ka?**
Do you want/like to go shopping again tomorrow?

Adakah anda hendak/suka pergi membeli-belah sekali lagi esok?

16. **Nani o kaitai desu ka?**
What do you want/like to buy?

Apakah yang anda suka/hendak beli?

17. **Jūkko tamago to, sanchaku fuku ga kaitai desu.**
I want/like to buy ten eggs and three dresses.

Saya suka/hendak membeli sepuluh biji telur dan tiga helai baju.

18. **Tēburu no shita ni nani ga arimasu ka?**
What is under the table?

Apakah yang ada di bawah meja itu?

19. **Tēburu no shita ni nihiki neko to ippiki inu ga imasu.**
There are two cats and one dog under the table.

Terdapat dua ekor kucing dan seekor anjing di bawah meja itu.

20. **Tana no ue ni nani ga arimasu ka?**
What is on top of the shelf?

Apakah yang ada di atas rak itu?

21. **Tana no ue ni sansatsu zasshi to shichihon pen ga arimasu.**
There are three magazines and seven pens on top of the shelf.

Terdapat tiga naskah majalah dan tujuh batang pen di atas rak itu.

22. **Dōbutsuen no naka ni nani ga imashita ka?**
What was inside the Zoo?

Apakah yang terdapat di dalam zoo itu?

23. **Dōbutsuen no naka ni hachihiki (happiki) sakana to, jup-**

Terdapat lapan ekor ikan, sepuluh ekor monyet, tujuh ekor ha-

piki saru to, nana to tora, san
to zō ga imashita.
There were eight fish, ten mon-
keys, seven tigers and three
elephants in the zoo.

*rimau dan tiga ekor gajah di
dalam zoo.*

24. **Ringo wa ikutsu arimasu ka?**
How many apples do you have?

Berapa biji epalkah anda ada?

25. **Hitotsu, futatsu, mitsu, yotsu**
...
One, two, three, four ...

Satu, dua, tiga, empat ...

26. **Ringo wa yotsu arimasu.**
I have four apples.

Saya ada empat biji epal.

27. **Nani ga hoshi desu ka?**
What do you want?

*Apakah yang awak mahu/hen-
dak?*

I. **Bunpō**
Grammar

Tatabahasa

(a) "Ue", "Shita", "Naka" etc.
Relative positions like on
top, under, inside etc. are
expressed in Japanese by
words such as "ue" (top),
"shita" (under), "naka" (inside) etc. These words are
usually followed by "ni" in
particular sentences.

*(a) "Ue", "Shita", "Naka" dan
sebagainya. Kedudukan rela-
tif seperti di atas, di bawah,
di dalam dan sebagainya di-
nyatakan di dalam Bahasa
Jepun dengan perkataan seperti "ue" (atas), "shita"
(bawah), "naka" (di dalam)
dan lain-lain. Perkataan-perkataan ini diikuti oleh "ni" di
dalam ayat-ayat tertentu.*

(i) **Hon wa hako no**
(ue)
(shita) } **ni arimashita.**
(naka)

*Ada beberapa buah buku di
(atas)
(bawah) } peti.
(dalam)*

There are several books
(on top of) ⎫
(under)   ⎬ the box.
(inside)   ⎭

(b) "Imasu" is the same as "arimasu" except that "arimasu" is usually used for things that cannot move while "imasu" is used for living things that move.

(b) *"Imasu" adalah sama dengan "arimasu" kecuali, "arimasu" selalu digunakan bagi benda-benda yang tidak boleh bergerak dan "imasu" pula digunakan bagi benda-benda yang hidup yang boleh bergerak.*

II. Dōshi   *Tatabahasa*
Grammar

Kata sekarang Present Tense ...masu	Bentuk kamus Dictionary Form ...u	Kemahuan Desire ...tai	Erti katakerja (Kata sekarang)
kaimasu buy	kau	kaitai want/like to buy	*beli*
urimasu sell	uru	uritai want/like to sell	*jual*
karimasu (i) borrow, (ii) to rent	kariru	(i) karitai (ii) want/like to borrow	*(i) pinjam (ii) sewa*
akemasu open	akeru	aketai want/like to open	*buka*
shimemasu close	shimeru	shimetai want/like to close	*tutup*
demasu to go out	deru	detai want/like to go out	*keluar*
owarimasu finish	owaru	owaritai want/like to finish	*tamat/habis*

ganbarimasu to do one's best	ganbaru	ganbaritai want/like to do one's best	*sebaik-baiknya*
iimasu say	iu	iitai want/like to say	*berkata/sebut*
haraimasu pay	harau	haraitai want/like to pay	*bayar*

A. *Berikan pengkelas yang sesuai untuk perkataan-perkataan di bawah ini.*
Give an appropriate classifier for the words below.

1. Eiga no kippu ga 2 arimasu.
   Eiga no kippu ga nimai arimasu.

2. Dōbutsuen de 3 tora, to 8 saru to 3 zō ga mimashita.

3. Enpitsu ga 6 to kami ga 5 kaitai desu.

4. Tēburu no ue ni hon ga 10 to kohi ga 3 arimasu.

5. Watashi wa inu ga 2 to neko ga 3 imasu.

6. Gakusei wa 10 imasu, 2 wa onna de, 8 wa otoko desu.

7. 2 kutsu to, 8 enpitsu ga kaitē kudasai.

8. Jidōsha ga 1 ikura desu ka?

9. Nan _____ ringo to tamago ga kaimashita ka?

10. 2 mizu o kudasai.

B. Give the classifiers for the following beginning with "How many" (Nan...).

Beri pengkelas bagi tempat-tempat kosong di bawah yang bermula dengan "berapa banyakkah" (Nan...).

1. Nan _____ hon ga arimasu ka?

2. Nan _____ kutsu ga kaimashita ka?

3. Nan _____ kocha o nomimashita ka?

4. Nan _____ inu o mimashita ka?

5. Nan _____ tora o imashita ka?

6. Nan _____ tamago o tabemashita ka?

7. Nan _____ fuku ga urimashita ka?

8. Nan _____ jidōsha ga moteimasu ka?

9. Fune ga nan _____ arimasu ka?

10. Hikoki ga nan _____ arimasu ka?

C. Fill in the blanks.   *Isikan tempat-tempat kosong.*

Bentuk kamus Dictionary Form	*Kemahuan* Desire
kau	
shiru	
deru	
	uritai
kaeru	
iku	
akeru	
konyaku suru	
	isogitai
okiru	

Pengkelas
Classifiers

	Benda Thing	*Orang* Persons	*Bijiran* Beans	*Benda-benda panjang misahnya:* pensel, botol. Long things e.g. pencil, bottle.	*Benda nipis misahnya:* kertas, pinggan. Thin things e.g. paper, plate.	*Benda-benda kecil misahnya:* telur, oren. Small things e.g. egg, orange.
1.	hitotsu	hitori	hitotsubu	ippon	ichimai	ikko
2.	futatsu	futari	fatatsubu	nihon	nimai	niko
3.	mittsu	sannin	mitsubu	sanbon	sanmai	sanko
4.	yottsu	yonin	yotsubu	yonhon	yonmai	yonko
5.	itsutsu	gonin	itsutsubu	gohon	gomai	goko
6.	muttsu	rokunin	mutsubu	roppon	rokumai	rokko
7.	nanatsu	nananin shichinin	nanatsubu	nanahon	nanamai	nanako
8.	yattsu	hachinin	yatsubu	happon	hachimai	hakko
9.	kokonotsu	kyūnin kunin	kokonotsubu	kyūhon	kyūmai	kyūko
10.	tō	jūnin	jitsubu	jūppon jippon	jūmai	jukko
11.	ikutsu	nannin	nantsubu	nanhoŋ	nanmai	nanko

	Binatang-binatang kecil misalnya: kucing/anjing. Small animals e.g. cat, dog.	*Binatang-binatang besar misalnya: harimau, kuda.* Big animals e.g. tiger, horse.	*Kasut, sarung kaki.* Shoes, socks, etc.	*Minuman dalam gelas.* Drinks which are in cups.	*Buku, majalah.* Books, magazines.	*Pakaian/Baju.* Dress.
1.	ippiki	ittō	issoku	ippai	issatsu	icchaku
2.	nihiki	nitō	nisoku	nihai	nisatsu	nichaku
3.	sanbiki	santō	sanzoku	sanbai	sansatsu	sanchaku
4.	yonhiki	yontō	yonsoku	yonhai	yonsatsu	yonchaku
5.	gohiki	gotō	gosoku	gohai	gosatsu	gochaku
6.	roppiki	rokutō	rokusoku	roppai	rokusatsu	rokuchaku
7.	shichihiki nanahiki	nanatō	nanasoku	nanahai	shichisatsu nanasatsu	shichichaku nanachaku
8.	hachihiki happiki	hachitō hattō	hassoku	happai	hassatsu	hachichaku hachaku
9.	kuhiki kyūhiki	kyūtō	kyūsoku	kyūhai	kyūsatsu	kyūchaku
10.	jippiki jūhiki	juttō	jūssoku	jūppai	jūssatsu	jichiaku jūcchaku
11.	nanbiki	nantō	nanzoku	nanbai	nansatsu	nanchaku

64

	Kapal terbang. Aeroplanes.	Kapal Ship.	Kenderaan. Vehicles.	Kekerapan (kali). Frequency. (no. of times).	Rumah. House.	Tingkat sebuah bangunan. Floor of a building.
1.	ikki	isseki	ichidai	ikkai (ichido)	ikken	ikkai
2.	niki	niseki	nidai	nikai	niken	nikai
3.	sanki	sanseki	sandai	sankai	sanken	sankai
4.	yonki	yonseki	yondai	yonkai	yonken	yonkai
5.	goki	goseki	godai	gokai	goken	gokai
6.	rokki	rokuseki	rokudai	rokkai	rokken	rokkai
7.	shichiki nanaki	nanaseki	shichidai	shichikai nanakai	nanaken	shichikai nanakai
8.	hachiki hakki	hasseki	hachidai	hachikai hakkai	hakken	hachikai hakkai
9.	kyūki	kyūseki	kyūdai	kyūkai	kyūken	kyūkai
10.	jikki	jūseki	jūdai	jikkai jūkkai	jūkken	jikkai jūkkai
11.	nanki	nanseki	nandai	nankai nando	nangen	nankai

Hombun Glossary	*Perbendaharaan kata*
1. **Mado** Window	*Tingkap*
2. **Doa** Door	*Pintu*
3. **Zasshi** Magazine	*Majalah*
4. **Onna** Girl	*Budak perempuan*
5. **Otoko** Boy	*Budak lelaki*
6. **Jōsei** Female	*Wanita*
7. **Dansei** Male	*Lelaki*
8. **Tēberu** Table	*Meja*
9. **Tsukue** Desk	*Meja kecil*
10. **Isu** Chair	*Kerusi*
11. **Tana** Shelf	*Rak*
12. **Heya** Room	*Bilik*
13. **Mame** Beans	*Bijiran*

14. **Tabako**
Cigarettes

Rokok

15. **Kami**
Paper

Kertas

16. **Chōmen**
Notebook

Buku nota

17. **Fune**
Ship

Kapal

18. **Hikoki**
Aeroplane

Kapal terbang

19. **Jidōsha**
Car

Kereta

20. **Jutan**
Carpet

Permaidani

21. **Todana**
Cupboard

Almari

22. **Kimono**
Clothing (Japanese)

Pakaian (Jepun)

23. **Yōfuku**
Clothing (western)

Pakaian (barat)

24. **Ue**
Top

Atas

25. **Naka**
Inside

Dalam

26. **Shita**
Under

Di bawah

27. **Soba**
Beside, by the side

Sebelah, disebelah

28. **Mae**   *Depan*
    Front

29. **Soto**   *Di luar*
    Outside

Daishichika - Hi, Shū, Gatsu
Pelajaran 7 - Hari, minggu, bulan (dalam sesuatu tahun)
Lesson 7 -- Days, Week, Month (of the year)

1. **Kyō wa nan nichi desu ka?**
   What is the date to-day?

   Apakah tarikh hari ini?

2. **Kyō wa mikka desu.**
   Today is the 3rd.

   Hari ini 3hb.

3. **Kinō wa nan nichi deshita ka?**
   What was the date yesterday?

   Apakah tarikh semalam?

4. **Kinō wa futsuka deshita.**
   Yesterday was the 2nd.

   Semalam 2hb.

5. **Ototoi wa nan nichi deshita ka?**
   What was the date the day before yesterday?

   Apakah tarikh kelmarin?

6. **Ashita wa nan yōbi desu ka?**
   What day (of the week) is tomorrow?

   Esok hari apa?

7. **Asatte wa nan yōbi desu ka?**
   What day (of the week) is the day after tomorrow?

   Lusa hari apa?

8. **Nichiyōbi wa nan nichi desu ka?**
   What date is Sunday?

   Apakah tarikh pada hari Ahad?

9. **Rai shū no getsuyōbi wa watashi no tanjōbi desu.**
   My birthday is next Monday.

   Hari jadi saya adalah pada hari Isnin depan.

10. **Sen shū no káyōbi wa kare no tanjōbi deshita.**
    His birthday was last Tuesday.

    Hari jadi beliau adalah pada hari Selasa lepas.

11. **Watashi no tanjōbi wa ichigatsu no jūgonichi ni desu.**
    My birthday is on the 15th of January.

    Hari jadi saya adalah pada 15hb Januari.

12. **Soshite, kare no tanjōbi wa rai shū no kinyōbi ni desu.**
    And his birthday is next Friday.

    Dan harijadi beliau adalah pada hari Jumaat depan.

13. **Fuyu wa jūnigatsu kara nigatsu made desu.**
    Winter is from December to (until) February.

    Musim dingin adalah dari bulan Disember hingga Februari.

14. **Sangatsu, shigatsu, gogatsu wa haru de, rokugatsu, shichigatsu, hachigatsu wa natsu desu.**
    March, April and May are Spring and June, July and August are Summer.

    Mac, April dan Mei adalah musim bunga dan Jun, Julai dan Ogos adalah musim panas.

15. **Aki wa kugatsu kara jūichigatsu made desu.**
    Autumn is from September to (until) December.

    Musim gugur adalah dari bulan September hingga Disember.

16. **Ichinen ni wa nankagetsu arimasu ka?**
    How many months are there in a year?

    Ada berapa bulan dalam satu tahun?

17. **Jūnikagetsu arimasu.**
    12 months.

    12 bulan.

18. **Natsu yasumi wa nankagetsu desu ka?**
    How many months is Summer vacation?

    Berapa bulankah cuti musim panas?

19. **Ikkagetsu ni wa sanjūnichi arimasu.**
    There are 30 days in a month.

    Ada 30 hari dalam satu bulan.

20. **Tsuki no hajime (saisho) no hi wa nan to iimasu ka?**
    What is the first day of the month called?

    Hari pertama dalam sesuatu bulan dipanggil apa?

21. **Tsuitachi (ichijitsu) to iimasu.**
    It is the 1st.

    Hari 1hb.

22. **Honto, desu ka?**
    Is it true?

    Adakah itu betul?

23. **Sō to omoimasu.**
    I think so.

    Saya fikir begitu.

24. **Rai nen no sangatsu wa yasumi to kikimashita.**
    I heard (that) next March is a holiday.

    Saya dengar bulan Mac tahun depan adalah cuti.

1. **Bunpō**
   Grammar

   Tatabahasa

   "No"
   (a) "No" is a Possessive Particle and means "of" or "'s"
       (i) **Kon shū no nichiyōbi wa watashi no tanjōbi desu.**

   "No" ialah Partikel Kepunyaan dan bermakna ".punya"

   Ahad ini harijadi saya.

This Sunday is my
birthday.

(ii) **Kare wa Taro san no**   *Beliau ialah guru En. Taro.*
sensei desu.
He is Mr. Taro's
teacher.

(b) "Kara" means "from".   *"Kara" bermakna "dari".*
Watashi wa Tōkyo kara   *Saya tidak datang dari Tokyo.*
kimasen deshita.
I did not come from Tokyo.

(c) "Kara" also denotes cause   *"Kara" juga menunjukkan*
or reason.   *sebab.*
Kyō wa yasumi deshita   *Oleh kerana hari ini hari cuti*
kara, Tōkyō ni ikimashita.   *saya telah pergi ke Tokyo.*
Because it was a holiday
today, I went to Tokyo.

2. **Dōshi**   *Katakerja*
   Verbs

Kata sekarang	Bentuk kamus	Bentuk jemputan (bolehkah kita)	Erti kerja (Kata sekarang)
Present Tense	Dictionary Form	Invitational (shall we)	
... masu	... u	... mashyoo (ka)	
kirimasu cut	kiru	kirimashyoo (ka) shall we cut	potong
naraimasu learn	narau	naraimashyoo (ka) shall we learn	belajar

machimasu wait	matsu	machimashyoo (ka) shall we wait	*tunggu*
sanpo shimasu stroll	sanpo suru	sanpo shimashyoo (ka) shall we (go for a) stroll	*bersiar-siar*
arukimasu walk	aruku	arukimashyoo (ka) shall we walk	*berjalan*
hashirimasu run	hashiru	hashirimashyoo (ka) shall we run	*lari*
tsukaimasu use	tsukau	tsukaimashyoo (ka) shall we use	*guna*
yasumimasu rest	yasumu	yasumimashyoo (ka) shall we rest	*rehat*
yobimasu call	yobu	yobimashyoo (ka) shall we call	*panggil*
hajimemasu begin	hajimeru	hajimemashyoo (ka) shall we begin	*mula*

A. Translate into Japanese.   *Terjemahkan dalam Bahasa Jepun.*

A: What day (of the week) is   *Hari ini hari apa?*

today?
B: Today is Tuesday.

Hari ini hari Selasa.

A: When is Mr. Tan's birthday?
B: It is next Monday.

Bilakah harijadi Encik Tan?
Pada Isnin depan.

A: What month is this?
B: It is August.

Bulan ini bulan apa?
Bulan Ogos.

A: What month is next month?
B: It is September.

Bulan depan bulan apa?
Bulan September.

A: What month was last month?
B: It was July.

Bulan lepas bulan apa?
Bulan Julai.

A: How many days are there in a week?
B: Seven days.

Ada berapa hari dalam seminggu?
Tujuh hari.

B. Fill in the blanks.

Isikan tempat-tempat kosong.

1. Nijūichinichi _____ sugi wa, nannichi _____ ka?

2. Ototoi _____ nannichi _____ ka?

3. Tsuki _____ hajime _____ hi _____ nan _____ iimasu ka?

4. Senshū _____ nichiyōbi _____ doko _____ ikimashita _____?

5. Ashita _____ kaisha ni imasu _____?

6. Asa _____ yūgata _____ ga hiruma desu.

7. Kayōbi _____ ishūkan _____ hajime _____ hi desu ka?

8. Watashi wa getsuyōbi _____ kinyōbi _____ hataraite, doyōbi _____ nichiyobi _____ yasumimasu.

9. Naze uchi _____ kimasen deshita ka?

10. Gobanme _____ hi _____ mokuyōbi de, rokubanme _____ hi _____ kinyōbi desu.

C. *Isikan tempat-tempat kosong.*
Fill in the blanks.

Bentuk kamus Dictionary form	Bentuk jemputan Invitational
sanpo suru	sanpo shimashyoo (ka)
iku	
hajimeru	
isogu	
kazoeru	
konyaku suru	
miru	
matsu	
kaku	
yobu	

Hombun
Glossary

Perbendaharaan kata

1. **Tsuitachi**
   1st (of the month)   *1hb*

2. **Futsuka**
   (i) 2nd of the month   *(i) 2hb*
   (ii) Two days   *(ii) Dua hari*

3. **Mikka**
   (i) 3rd of the month   *(i) 3hb*
   (ii) Three days   *(ii) Tiga hari*

4. **Yokka**
   (i) 4th of the month   (i) *4hb*
   (ii) Four days   (ii) *Empat hari*

5. **Itsuka**
   (i) 5th of the month   (i) *5hb*
   (ii) Five days   (ii) *Lima hari*

6. **Muika**
   (i) 6th of the month   (i) *6hb*
   (ii) Six days   (ii) *Enam hari*

7. **Nanoka**
   (i) 7th of the month   (i) *7hb*
   (ii) Seven days   (ii) *Tujuh hari*

8. **Yōka**
   (i) 8th of the month   (i) *8hb*
   (ii) Eight days   (ii) *Lapan hari*

9. **Kokonoka**
   (i) 9th of the month   (i) *9hb*
   (ii) Nine days   (ii) *Sembilan hari*

10. **Tōka**
   (i) 10th of the month   (i) *10hb*
   (ii) Ten days   (ii) *Sepuluh hari*

11. **Jūichinichi**
   (i) 11th of the month   (i) *11hb*
   (ii) Eleven days   (ii) *Sebelas hari*

12. **Jūninichi**
   (i) 12th of the month   (i) *12hb*
   (ii) Twelve days   (ii) *Dua belas hari*

13. **Jūsannichi**
   (i) 13th of the month   (i) *13hb*

(ii) Thirteen days	(ii) Tiga belas hari

14. Jūyokka

(i) 14th of the month	(i) 14hb
(ii) Fourteen days	(ii) Empat belas hari

15. Jūgonichi

(i) 15th of the month	(i) 15hb
(ii) Fifteen days	(ii) Lima belas hari

16. Jūrokunichi

(i) 16th of the month	(i) 16hb
(ii) Sixteen days	(ii) Enam belas hari

17. Jūshichinichi

(i) 17th of the month	(i) 17hb
(ii) Seventeen days	(ii) Tujuh belas hari

18. Jūhachinichi

(i) 18th of the month	(i) 18hb
(ii) Eighteen days	(ii) Lapan belas hari

19. Jūkunichi

(i) 19th of the month	(i) 19hb
(ii) Nineteen days	(ii) Sembilan belas hari

20. Hatsuka

(i) 20th of the month	(i) 20hb
(ii) Twenty days	(ii) Dua puluh hari

21. Nijūichinichi

(i) 21st of the month	(i) 21hb
(ii) Twenty-one days	(ii) Dua puluh satu hari

22. Nijūninichi

(ii) 22nd of the month	(i) 22hb
(ii) Twenty-two days	(ii) Dua puluh dua hari

23. **Nijūsannichi**
   (i) 23rd of the month   *(i) 23hb*
   (ii) Twenty-three days   *(ii) Dua puluh tiga hari*

24. **Nijūyokka**
   (i) 24th of the month   *(i) 24hb*
   (ii) Twenty-four days   *(ii) Dua puluh empat hari*

25. **Nijūgonichi**
   ʼ(i) 25th of the month   *(i) 25hb*
   (ii) Twenty-five days   *(ii) Dua puluh lima hari*

26. **Nijūrokunichi**
   (i) 26th of the month   *(i) 26hb*
   (ii) Twenty-six days   *(ii) Dua puluh enam hari*

27. **Nijūshichinichi**
   (i) 27th of the month   *(i) 27hb*
   (ii) Twenty-seven days   *(ii) Dua puluh tujuh hari*

28. **Nijūhachinichi**
   (i) 28th of the month   *(i) 28hb*
   (ii) Twenty-eight days   *(ii) Dua puluh lapan hari*

29. **Nijūkunichi**
   (i) 29th of the month   *(i) 29hb*
   (ii) Twenty-nine days   *(ii) Dua puluh sembilan hari*

30. **Sanjūnichi**
   (i) 30th of the month   *(i) 30hb*
   (ii) Thirty days   *(ii) Tiga puluh hari*

31. **Sanjūichinichi**
   (i) 31st of the month   *(i) 31hb*
   (ii) Thirty-one days   *(ii) Tiga puluh satu hari*

32. **Nannichi desu ka?**
   What day (of the month) is it?   *Hari ini berapa haribulan?*

33. **Ishūkan**
   One week

   Satu minggu

34. **Nishūkan**
   Two weeks

   Dua minggu

35. **Sanshūkan**
   Three weeks

   Tiga minggu

36. **Yonshūkan**
   Four weeks

   Empat minggu

37. **Goshūkan**
   Five weeks

   Lima minggu

38. **Rokushūkan**
   Six weeks

   Enam minggu

39. **Shichishūkan (Nanashūkan)**
   Seven weeks

   Tujuh minggu

40. **Hashūkan**
   Eight weeks

   Lapan minggu

41. **Kyūshūkan**
   Nine weeks

   Sembilan minggu

42. **Jūshūkan**
   Ten weeks

   Sepuluh minggu

43. **Nanshūkan desu ka?**
   How many weeks?

   Berapa minggu?

44. **Ichigatsu**
   January

   Januari

45. **Nigatsu**
   February

   Februari

46. **Sangatsu** March	*Mac*
47. **Shigatsu** April	*April*
48. **Gogatsu** May	*Mei*
49. **Rokugatsu** June	*Jun*
50. **Shichigatsu** July	*Julai*
51. **Hachigatsu** August	*Ogos*
52. **Kugatsu** September	*September*
53. **Jūgatsu** October	*Oktober*
54. **Jūichigatsu** November	*November*
55. **Jūnigatsu** December	*Disember*
56. **Nangatsu desu ka?** What month is it?	*Ini bulan apa?*
57. **Ikkagetsu** One month	*Satu bulan*
58. **Nikagetsu** Two months	*Dua bulan*

59. **Sankagetsu**   *Tiga bulan*
   Three months

60. **Yonkagetsu**   *Empat bulan*
   Four months

61. **Gokagetsu**   *Lima bulan*
   Five months

62. **Rokkagetsu**   *Enam bulan*
   Six months

63. **Shichikagetsu (Nanakagetsu)**   *Tujuh bulan*
   Seven months

64. **Hachikagetsu**   *Lapan bulan*
   Eight months

65. **Kyūkagetsu**   *Sembilan bulan*
   Nine months

66. **Jūkkagetsu**   *Sepuluh bulan*
   Ten months

67. **Nankagetsu desu ka?**   *Berapa bulan?*
   How many months?

68. **Ichinen**   *Satu tahun*
   One year

69. **Ninen**   *Dua tahun*
   Two years

70. **Sannen**   *Tiga tahun*
   Three years

71. **Yonen**   *Empat tahun*
   Four years

72. **Gonen**
    Five years
    Lima tahun

73. **Rokunen**
    Six years
    Enam tahun

74. **Shichinen, Nananen**
    Seven years
    Tujuh tahun

75. **Hachinen**
    Eight years
    Lapan tahun

76. **Kyūnen**
    Nine years
    Sembilan tahun

77. **Jūnen**
    Ten years
    Sepuluh tahun

78. **Nanen desu ka?**
    How many years?
    Berapa tahun?

79. **Kisetsu**
    Season
    Musim

80. **Haru**
    Spring
    Musim bunga

81. **Natsu**
    Summer
    Musim panas

82. **Aki**
    Autumn
    Musim gugur

83. **Fuyu**
    Winter
    Musim dingin

84. **Kanki**
    Dry season
    Musim kemarau

85. **Uki** *Musim hujan*
Rainy season

86. **Kashi** *Fahrenheit*
Fahrenheit

87. **Sesshi** *Centigrade*
Centigrade

88. **Taionkei** *Jangka suhu klinik*
Thermometer (clinical)

89. **Kandankei** *Jangka suhu*
Thermometer

90. **Yasumi** · *Cuti*
Holiday

91. **Kyō** *Hari ini*
Today

92. **Kinō** *Semalam*
Yesterday

93. **Ototoi** *Kelmarin*
Day before yesterday

94. **Ashita** *Esok*
Tomorrow

95. **Asatte** *Lusa*
Day after tomorrow

96. **Konshū** *Minggu ini*
This week

97. **Raishū** *Minggu depan*
Next week

98.	**Senshū** Last week	*Minggu lepas*
99.	**Kongetsu** This month	*Bulan ini*
100.	**Raigetsu** Next month	*Bulan depan*
101.	**Sengetsu** Last month	*Bulan lepas*
102.	**Kotoshi** This year	*Tahun ini*
103.	**Rainen** Next year	*Tahun depan*
104.	**Kyōnen** Last year	*Tahun lepas*
105.	**Karendā** Calendar	*Kalender*
106.	**Getsumatsu** Month end	*Hujung bulan*
107.	**Taiyō-** Sun	*Matahari*
108.	**Tsuki** Moon	*Bulan*
109.	**Hoshi** Star	*Bintang*
110.	**Tsumetai** Cold	*Sejuk*

111. **Suzushii**   *Sejuk (dingin)*
     Cool

112. **Atatakai**   *Hangat*
     Warm

113. **Taifu**   *Angin taufan*
     Typhoon

114. **Jishin**   *Gempa bumi*
     Earthquake

115. **Ōame**   *Hujan lebat*
     Heavy rain

116. **Kosame**   *Hujan renyai-renyai*
     Light rain

117. **Ōmizu**   *Banjir*
     Flood

Daihakka – Fukushū
Pelajaran 8 – Latihan Ulangkaji
Lesson 8 – Review Exercises

A. *Padankan perkataan-perkataan berikut:*
Match the following:

1. *Selamat pagi.*
   Good morning.

   a. **Sumimasen.**

2. *Selamat tengahari.*
   Good afternoon.

   b. **Dō itashimashite.**

3. *Selamat petang.*
   Good evening.

   c. **Chotto matte kudasai.**

4. *Terima kasih.*
   Thank you.

   d. **Hai, genki desu.**

5. *Selamat tinggal.*
   Good-bye.

   e. **Ogenki desu ka?**

6. *Apa khabar?*
   How are you?

   f. **Sayonara.**

7. *Khabar baik.*
   I am well.

   g. **Dōmo arigatō gozaimasu.**

8. *Minta maaf.*
   Excuse me.

   h. **Konban wa.**

9. *Sama-sama (terima kasih).*
   Please don't mention.

   i. **Konnichi wa.**

10. *Tolong tunggu sebentar.*
    Just a moment, please.

    j. **Ohayō gozaimasu.**

86

B. *Padankan rangkaikata-rangkaikata berikut:*
   Match the following:

1. *Sila duduk.*   a. **Nihongo o naraimashita.**
   Please sit.

2. *Minta maaf kerana saya*   b. **Kurikaeshite kudasai.**
   terlambat.
   Sorry to keep you waiting.

3. *Selamat Tahun Baru.*   c. **Yoku dekimashita.**
   Happy New Year.

4. *Sila lihat itu bersama-sama.*   d. **Shinen omedetō**
   Please look at it together.   **gozaimasu.**

5. *Tolong tuliskan sekali lagi.*   e. **Dōzo okake kudasai.**
   Please write it once more.

6. *Anda melakukan dengan*   f. **Hai, wakarimashıta.**
   baik.
   You did well.

7. *Tolong ulang.*   g. **Omatase shimashita.**
   Please repeat.

8. *Ya, saya telah faham.*   h. **Nihongo o oshiemashita.**
   Yes, I understood.

9. *Saya telah belajar Bahasa*   i. **Mō ichido kaite kudasai.**
   Jepun.
   I learned the Japanese
   language.

10. *Saya telah mengajar*   j. **Isshoni mite kudasai.**
    bahasa Jepun.
    I taught the Japanese
    language.

C. *Susunkan perkataan-perkataan dalam ayat di bawah untuk dijadikannya ayat yang betul.*
Reconstruct the following sentences correctly.

1. wa Nihon go o watashi narateimasu

2. desu wa kore ka nan

3. ka wa kinō deshita atsui

4. doko ka ni sundeimasu wa anata

5. sensei wa desu no watashi konokata

6. kara ichigatsu Nihon ni watashi sangatsu made wa ikimashita ni

7. desu nanyōbi ka ashita wa

8. nannichi ni ichi arimasu nen ka

9. arimasen wa Nihon go ja muzukashii

10. Nihon kare senshū wa ikimashita ni

D. *Tukarkan ayat-ayat berikut ke dalam Bahasa Jepun.*
Change the following sentences into Japanese.

1. *Apa ini?*
   What is this?

2. *Bolehkah anda bercakap Bahasa Jepun?*
   Do you speak Japanese?

3. *Di manakah anda berkerja?*
   Where do you work?

4. *Bilakah anda berkahwin?*
   When did you marry?

5. *Mengapakah anda belajar Bahasa Jepun?*
   Why do you study the Japanese language?

6. *Minggu lepas saya pergi ke Jepun.*
   Last week I went to Japan.

7. *Pukul berapa sekarang?*
   What is the time now?

8. *Hari ini hari apa?*
   What day (of the week) is today?

9. *Hari jadi saya adalah pada 4hb Januari.*
   My birthday is on 4th January.

10. *Bolehkah kita bertemu esok?*
    Shall we meet tomorrow?

E. *Apa yang anda akan katakan dalam bahasa Jepun bila:*
   What would you say in Japanese when:

1. *Anda lambat.*
   You are late.

2. *Anda menyuruh seseorang itu duduk.*
   You ask someone to sit.

3. *Anda meminta seseorang supaya mengulang apa yang baru dikatakannya.*
   You ask someone to repeat what he has just said.

4. *Anda meminta seseorang menunggu sebentar.*
   You ask someone to wait for a while.

5. *Anda memerlukan seseorang untuk bercakap dengan kuat, apa yang baru sahaja dikatakannya.*
   You want someone to repeat what he has just said, louder.

F. *Jelaskan yang berikut dalam bahasa Jepun:*
Express the following in Japanese:

1. 10

2. 13

3. 17

4. 21

5. 31

6. 274

7. 326

8. 1000

9. *5.05 pagi*
5.05 a.m.

10. *2.30 tengahari*
2.30 p.m.

11. *8.15 pagi*
8.15 a.m.

12. *10 minit lagi pukul 8.*
10 minutes to 8.

13. *12 minit lagi pukul 6.*
12 minutes to 6.

14. *Isnin*
Monday

15. *Rabu*
Wednesday

16. *Jumaat*
Friday

17. *Sabtu*
Saturday

18. *April*
April

19. *Mei*
May

20. *Oktober*
October

21. *Disember*
December

22. *1 haribulan*
1st day of the month

23. *3hb*
3rd day of the month

24. *10hb*
10th day of the month

25. *20hb*
20th day of the month

26. *27hb*
27th day of the month

27. *Satu bulan*
One month

28. *Lima bulan*
Five months

90

29. *Tujuh bulan*
    Seven months

30. *Sepuluh bulan*
    Ten months

G. *Isikan tempat-tempat kosong.*
   Fill in the blanks.

Kata sekarang Present Tense	*Bentuk kamus* Dictionary Form	*Kata lampau* Past Tense	*Kata lampau (negatif)* Past Negative	*Keinginan* Desire
wakarimasu				
		ikimashita		
				benkyō shitai
	miru			
			kikimasen deshita	
nemasu				
		kaerimashita		
			demasen deshita	
				owaritai
sanpo shimasu				
		arukimashita		
	hashiru			
			hajimemasen deshita	
				haraitai
	kau			

Daikyūka - Nichijō Seikatsu
Pelajaran 9 - Kehidupan Harian
Lesson 9 - Daily Life

1. **Watashi wa maiasa goji goro ni okimasu.**
   I get up at about 5 a.m. everyday.

   Saya bangun kira-kira pada pukul 5 pagi setiap hari.

2. **Okite kara ha o migaite, kao o araite, hige o sorimasu.**
   After getting up, I brush my teeth, wash my face and shave.

   Selepas bangun, saya menggosok gigi, mencuci muka dan mencukur.

3. **Hachiji ni asagohan o tabete, kaisha ni ikimasu.**
   I eat breakfast at 8 o'clock and then go to my company.

   Saya makan sarapan pagi pada pukul 8.00 pagi dan kemudian pergi ke syarikat saya.

4. **Kaisha ni basu de ikimasu.**
   I go to my company by bus.

   Saya pergi ke syarikat saya dengan bas.

5. **Tokidoki aruite ikimasu.**
   Sometimes I walk.

   Kadang-kadang saya berjalan kaki.

6. **Watashi wa gishi desu.**
   I am an engineer.

   Saya seorang jurutera.

7. **Watashi wa kekkon shite, kodomo ga sannin imasu.**
   I am married and have three children.

   Saya sudah berkahwin dan mempunyai tiga orang anak.

8. **Hiru made hataraite kara, hirugohan o tabemasu.**
   After working until noon, I take (eat) lunch.

   Selepas bekerja sehingga tengahari, saya makan makanan tengahari.

9. **Hiru yasumi wa jūniji kara ichiji made desu.**
   Lunch-break is from 12 to 1 o'clock.

   Masa makan tengahari ialah dari pukul 12.00 hingga 1.00.

10. **Uchi kara obentō o motte ikimasu.**
    I take my lunch from home.

    Saya membawa makan tengahari dari rumah.

11. **Ichiji ni shigoto o suzukete, yūgata made hatarakimasu.**
    I resume work at one o'clock and work till evening.

    Saya terus bekerja pada pukul satu sehingga petang.

12. **Tokidoki zangyō ga arimasu (aru) kara, osoku made hatarakimasu.**
    Sometimes since there is overtime work, I work late.

    Kadang-kadang, oleh kerana ada kerja masa tambahan, saya kerja sehingga lewat petang.

13. **Uchi ni kaete kara ofuro o hairimasu (shawā o abimasu).**
    After returning home I take a bath (take a shower).

    Setelah pulang ke rumah, saya mandi.

14. **Sore kara rajio o kitari, terebi o mitari, hon o yondari shimasu.**
    And then I listen to the radio, see T.V. or read books.

    Kemudian, saya mendengar radio, menonton televisyen dan membaca buku.

15. **Doyōbi wa hannichi kara, tomodachi to asobi ni ikimasu.**

    Oleh kerana hari Sabtu adalah kerja setengah hari, saya keluar

Since Saturday is a half day, I go out with friends.

(untuk bersuka ria) dengan kawan-kawan.

16. **Tomodachi to kaimono shitari, eiga o mitari shimasu.**
I go shopping, and see movies with (my) friends.

Saya membeli belah dan menonton wayang gambar dengan kawan-kawan (saya).

17. **Osoku made asobu kara, taihen tsukaremasu.**
Since I am out until late (at night), I am very tired.

Oleh kerana saya bersuka ria sampai lewat malam, saya berasa sangat letih.

1. **Bunpō**
Grammar

Tatabahasa

(a) "Goro" and "Gurai".
The particle "goro" means "about". But it is usually used to denote time.

(Ichi) ji goro desu.
About one o'clock.

*"Goro" dan "Gurai".
Partikel "goro" bermakna kira-kira. Tetapi ianya biasa digunakan untuk menandakan masa.*

Kira-kira pukul satu.

(b) "Gurai" also means "about". Other meanings are "as much as".
Kono hon wa gohyaku en gurai desu.
This book costs about 500 yen.

*"Gurai" juga bermakna "kira-kira". Erti lain ialah "sebanyak-banyaknya".
Buku ini berharga kira-kira 500 yen.*

(c) "... Te Kara"
Denotes "after" and it is usually preceded by a verb, e.g. tabete kara (after eating), nonde kara (after drinking).

*"... Te Kara"
Menandakan "selepas" dan ini selalunya diikuti oleh perbuatan, contohnya, **tabete kara** (selepas makan), **nonde kara** (selepas minum).*

Tabete kara eiga o mimashita.	*Setelah makan, saya menonton wayang.*	
After eating, I saw a movie.		

2. Dōshi
Verbs

Katakerja

Kata sekarang Present Tense	Bentuk kamus Dictionary Form	Kata sekarang (*berterusan*) Present Continuous	Erti katakerja (*Kata sekarang*)
... **masu**	... **u**	... **teimasu** ... **deimasu**	
sawarimasu touch	**sawaru**	**sawatteimasu**	*sentuh*
migakimasu brush, polish	**migaku**	**migaiteimasu**	*berus, mengilat*
araimasu wash	**arau**	**aratteimasu**	*cuci*
motte ikimasu bring	**motte iku**	**motte itteimasu**	*membawa*
suzukemasu continue	**suzukeru**	**suzuketeimasu**	*sambung*
asobimasu play	**asobu**	**asondeimasu**	*main*
oyogimasu swim	**oyugu**	**oyondeimasu**	*berenang*
ugokimasu move	**ugoku**	**ugoiteimasu**	*gerak*
nugimasu take off (clothes)	**nugu**	**nuideimasu**	*tanggal (pakaian)*
torimasu take	**toru**	**totteimasu**	*ambil*

A. *Jawap soalan-soalan yang berikut.*
Answer the following questions.

A: **Anata wa mainichi nanji ni okimasu ka?**
B:

A: **Nanji ni asagohan o tabemasu ka?**
B:

A: **Kaisha de nani o shimasu ka?**
B:

A: **Hiru yasumi wa nanji kara nanji made desu ka?**
B:

A: **Doyōbi wa hannichi desu ka?**
B:

A: **Nichiyōbi wa nani o shimasu ka?**
B:

A: **Ima wa nani o shiteimasu ka?**
B:

B. Change these sentences into Japanese.

    Tukarkan ayat-ayat ini kepada Bahasa Jepun.

1. I get up at 7 a.m. everyday.
    Saya bangun pada pukul 7.00 pagi setiap hari.

2. After I get up, I brush my teeth.
    Selepas saya bangun, saya menggosok gigi.

3. Sometimes I work until late.
    Kadangkala saya bekerja sehingga lewat malam.

4. I read books, see movies and do shopping.
    Saya membaca buku, menonton wayang dan membeli-belah.

5. Sometimes I go to my company by bus.
    Kadangkala, saya pergi ke syarikat saya dengan bas.

6. When I return home, I take a bath.

Selepas saya balik ke rumah saya mandi.

7. I work everyday.

Saya bekerja setiap hari.

8. Because I work hard, I am tired.

Oleh kerana saya bekerja kuat saya berasa letih.

9. How much is your salary?

Berapa banyakkah gaji awak?

10. I did not brush my teeth today.

Saya tidak menggosok gigi hari ini.

C. *Susun kembali ayat-ayat berikut.*
Rearrange the following sentences.

1. okimasu mainichi ni wa rokuji.

2. desu kara hiru wa ka nanji yasumi.

3. shimasu o wa ka nani ima.

4. ga nichiyōbi yasumi doyōbi desu to.

5. nanji nemasu maiban goro ka wa ni.

Hombun
Glossary

Perbendaharaan kata

1. **Mainichi**
Every day

Setiap hari

2. **Maishu**
Every night

Setiap malam

3. **Maigetsu**
Every month

Setiap bulan

4. **Maiasa**
Every morning

Setiap pagi

5. **Maiban**
Every night

Setiap malam

6. **Okimasu**
Get up

Bangun

7. **Tokidoki**
Sometimes

Sekali sekala (kadang-kadang)

8. **Itsumo**
Always

Sering (selalu)

9. **Shachō**
President (of a company)

Pengerusi (sebuah syarikat)

10. **Buchō**
Manager

Pengurus

11. **Kacho**
Section chief

Ketua seksi (bahagian)

12. **Gishi**
Engineer

Jurutera

13. **Isha**
Doctor

Doktor

14. **Jimuin**
Office worker

Pekerja pejabat

15. **Jimusho**
Office

Pejabat

16. **Shain**
Company employees

Kakitangan syarikat

17. **Ginkō**
Bank

Bank

18. **Ginkōka**
Banker

Pekerja bank

19. **Untenshu** Driver	*Pemandu*
20. **Haiyū** Film star	*Bintang filem*
21. **Danyū** Actor	*Pelakon lelaki*
22. **Jōyū** Actress	*Pelakon wanita*
23. **Kashu** Singer	*Penyanyi*
24. **Tsūyakusha** Interpreter	*Penterjemah*
25. **Kōmuin** Civil servant	*Pekerja kerajaan*
26. **Hisho** Secretary	*Setiausaha*
27. **Rōdosha** Labourer	*Buruh*
28. **Shufu** Housewife	*Suri rumahtangga*
29. **Kōjō** Factory	*Kilang*
30. **Jugyōin** Factory workers	*Pekerja-pekerja kilang*
31. **Jitsugyōka** Businessmen	*Ahli perniagaan*
32. **Bengoshi** Lawyer	*Peguam*

33. **Yoku**
Well

Jadi

34. **Kitto**
Surely

Pasti

35. **Tabun**
Perhaps

Mungkin

36. **Zuibun**
Considerably

Pertimbangan

37. **Zehi**
By all means

Dipersilakan

38. **Totemo**
Taihen
Very

Sangat

39. **Sugu**
Soon

Tidak lama lagi

40. **Hotondo**
· Almost

Hampir

41. **Taitei**
Mostly

Kebanyakan

42. **Futsu**
Usually, Commonly

Selalunya, Kerapnya

43. **Sorekara**
And then

Kemudian

44. **Araimasu**
Wash

Cuci

45. **Sorimasu**
Share

Cukur

46. **Hige**
Moustache

Misai

47. **Osoi**
Late

Lambat, Lewat

48. **Ofuro**
Bath

Tempat mandi

49. **Rajio**
Radio

Radio

50. **Terebi**
Television

Televisyen

51. **Eiga**
Movie

Wayang

52. **Asobimasu**
To enjoy

Bersuka ria

53. **Jōbu**
Strong, healthy

Kuat, sihat

Daijūkka – Kaimono
Pelajaran 10 – Membeli-belah
Lesson 10 – Shopping

1. **Anata wa kinō nani o shimashita ka?**
   What did you do yesterday?

   Apakah anda buat semalam?

2. **Depāto ni ikimashita.**
   I went to a departmental store.

   Saya pergi ke pusat membeli-belah.

3. **Dono depāto ni ikimashita ka?**
   Which departmental store did you go to?

   Pusat membeli-belah yang mana anda pergi?

4. **Kimisawa ni ikimashita.**
   I went to Kimisawa.

   Saya telah pergi ke Kimisawa.

5. **Depāto ni wa iroirona mono ga arimashita.**
   There were various things in the departmental store.

   Terdapat berbagai jenis barang di pusat membeli-belah.

6. **Kore wa shatsu no uriba de, sore wa kutsushita no uriba desu.**
   This is the shirt counter and that is the socks counter.

   Ini adalah kaunter kemeja dan itu pula adalah kaunter sarung kaki.

7. **Nani o sashi agemashyoo ka?**
   What can I do for you?

   Apa yang boleh saya buat untuk anda?

8. **Tetsudate agemashyoo ka?**
   Can I help you?

   Bolehkah saya tolong anda?

9. **Watashi wa shatsu ga kaitai desu.**
   I want to buy a shirt.

   Saya ingin membeli kemeja.

10. **Shatsu o misete kudasai.**
Please show me some shirts.

Tolong tunjukkan saya kemeja.

11. **Ōkii shatsu to chiisai shatsu ga arimasu.**
There are big and small shirts.

Terdapat kemeja yang besar dan kecil.

12. **Soshite akai shatsu to shiroi shatsu mo arimasu.**
These are also red and white shirts.

Ada juga kemeja yang merah dan yang putih.

13. **Dōzo mite kudasai.**
Please have a look.

Tolong lihat.

14. **Dochira ga suki desu ka, shiroi shatsu to akai shatsu desu ka?**
Which do you like, the white or red shirt?

Yang manakah anda suka, baju putih atau baju merah?

15. **Are ga hoshii desu.**
I want that one (the one over there).

Saya mahu yang itu.

16. **Sore wa kini irimasen. Hokano ga hoshii desu.**
This does not interest me. I'd like a different one.

Saya tidak tertarik dengan ini. Saya inginkan yang lain.

17. **Kore wa do desu ka?**
What about this?

Bagaimana dengan yang ini?

18. **Kono iro wa suki ja arimasen.**
I don't like this colour.

Saya tidak suka warna ini.

19. **Motto akarui iro ga suki desu.**
I'd like a lighter colour.

Saya suka warna yang lebih cerah.

20. **Kono kireina shatsu wa ikura desu ka?**
How much is this beautiful shirt?

Berapakah harga kemeja yang cantik ini?

21. Kono shatsu wa ōki desu ne?
This shirt is large, isn't it?

Baju ini besar, bukankah begitu?

22. Moto chiisai no o kudasai.
Please give me a smaller one.

Tolong berikan saya yang lebih kecil.

23. Akai shatsu wa ichimai ikura desu ka?
How much is a red shirt?

Berapakah harga satu kemeja merah?

24. Gosen (5,000) en desu.
It is 5,000 yen.

Ia adalah 5,000 yen.

25. Takasugimasu ne!
Chotto makete kudasai.
It is too expensive (isn't it?).
Please reduce (the price) a bit.

Ia terlalu mahal (bukankah begitu?).
Tolong kurangkan (harga) sedikit.

26. Sumimasen, teika dōri de gozaimasu.
I am sorry, all prices are fixed.

Maafkan saya, semuanya harga tetap.

27. Doko de shiharai desu ka?
Where do I pay?

Di mana harus saya bayar?

28. Soko no chōba de harate kudasai.
Please pay at that counter.

Tolong bayar di kaunter itu.

29. Kore o kirei ni tsutsunde kudasai.
Please pack this up nicely.

Tolong bungkuskan ini dengan baik.

30. Hai, kashikomarimashita.
Yes Sir, I will.

Baik tuan.

31. Watashi no ie (uchi) ni todokete kudasai.
Please send it to my house.

Tolong hantarkannya ke rumah saya.

32. **Chotto matte kudasai.**   *Tolong tunggu sebentar.*
    Just a moment, please.

33. **Dōmo arigato gozaimashita.**   *Terima kasih.*
    Thank you.

34. **Mata dōzo.**   *Sila datang lagi.*
    Please come again.

1. **Bunpō**   *Tatabahasa*
   Grammar

(a) "Mo" denotes something   *"Mo" menandakan adanya*
    additional and means "also"   *sesuatu tambahan dan juga*
    and "too" in English.   *bermakna "juga" dalam Bahasa*
    Malaysia.
    Watashi mo sensei desu.   *Saya juga seorang guru atau*
    I am also a teacher or I am a   *saya seorang guru juga.*
    teacher too.

(b) "Mo" can also be used in a   *"Mo" boleh juga digunakan*
    negative sentence.   *dalam ayat negatif.*
    Kare mo sensei ja arimasen.   *Dia juga bukan seorang guru.*
    He is not a teacher either.

(c) "Mo" can also be used with   *"Mo" boleh juga digunakan*
    a negative expression.   *dalam ekspresi yang negatif.*
    (i) **Nani mo arimasen.**   *Tidak ada apapun.*
        There is nothing.
    (ii) **Nani ka imasu ka?**   *Adakah apa-apa?*
        Is there anything?
        Iie, nani mo imasen.   *Tidak, tiada apa-apa.*
        No, there is nothing.
    (iii) **Dare ka imasu ka?**   *Adakah sesiapa di situ?*
        Is there anyone?
        Iie, dare mo imasen.   *Tidak, tiada sesiapa.*
        No, there is no one.

2. Dōshi   Katakerja
Verbs

Kata sekarang Present Tense ... masu	Bentuk kamus Dictionary Form ... u	Bentuk suruhan (halus) Please (Polite) Form ... te kudasai ... de kudasai	Erti katakerja (Kata sekarang)
iremasu put into	ireru	irete kudasai please put into	memasukkan ke dalam
agemasu give	ageru	agete kudasai please give	beri
uchimasu to strike	utsu	utte kudasai please strike	pukul
tetsudaimasu to help	tetsudau	tetsudate kudasai please help	tolong
misemasu to show	miseru	misete kudasai please show	tunjuk
makemasu to reduce	makeru	makete kudasai please reduce	kurangkan
kachimasu to win	katsu	katte kudasai please win	menang
tachimasu stand, build	tatsu	tatte kudasai please stand, please build	berdiri, bina
wasuremasu forget	wasureru	wasurete kudasai please forget	lupa
todokemasu despatch	todokeru	todokete kudasai please despatch	hantar

A. **Mijikai kaiwa.**
A Short Conversation.

Satu perbualan pendek.

Please continue the conversation. Please discuss the price and ask the shop assistant for a reduction.

Tolong teruskan perbualan. Tolong tawarkan harga dan minta pembantu kedai untuk potongan harga.

A: **Irrashaimase, Nani o sashi agemashyoo ka?**

B: **Kamera ga hoshii desu.**

A: **Hai, iroiro wa gozaimasu.**
   Kore wa do desu ka?

A: **Ikura desu ka?**

B. *Buat ayat dengan perkataan-perkataan berikut.*
Make sentences with the following words.

(1) **misete kudasai**

(2) **makete kudasai**

(3) **wasuremasu**

(4) **todokete kudasai**

(5) **nani mo**

(6) **dare mo**

(7) **ikura**

(8) **iremasu**

(9) **motte ikimasu**

(10) **uriba**

C. Fill in the blanks.   *Isikan tempat-tempat kosong.*

Bentuk kamus Dictionary form.	Bentuk suruhan (halus) Please (polite) form.
yomu	
tatsu	
todokeru	
nomu	
yobu	
oyogu	
miru	
makeru	
kiku	
kaku	

Hombun
Glossary

Perbendaharaan kata

1. **Shatsu**
   Shirt

   Kemeja (baju)

2. **Kutsu**
   Shoes

   Kasut

3. **Kutsushita**
   Stockings

   Sarung kaki

4. **Kamera**
   Camera

   Kamera

5. **Omocha**
   Toys

   Barang permainan kanak-kanak

6. **Nekutai**
   Necktie

   Tali leher

7. **Seeta**
Sweater

Kemeja kain panas

8. **Bōshi**
Hat

Topi

9. **Kasa**
Umbrella

Payung

10. **Keshoin**
Cosmetics

Alat persolekan

11. **Megane**
Spectacles

Cermin mata

12. **Hōseki**
Jewellery

Barang kemas

13. **Yubiwa**
Ring

Cincin

14. **Ikura?**
How much?

Berapa banyak?

15. **Fūto**
Envelope

Sampul surat

16. **Binsen**
Writing pad

Buku kertas tulisan

17. **Mise**
Shop

Kedai

18. **Chiisai**
Small

Kecil

19. **Takai**
Expensive, Tall

Mahal, Tinggi

20. **Kaban**
Bag

Beg

21.	**Shinju** Pearl	*Mutiara*
22.	**Kin** Gold	*Emas*
23.	**Gin** Silver	*Perak*
24.	**Yasui** Cheap	*Murah*
25.	**Iroiro** Various	*Berbagai jenis*
26.	**Iro** Colour	*Warna*
27.	**Nuno, Kire** Cloth	*Kain*
28.	**Ke** Wool	*Bulu kambing*
29.	**Kinu** Silk	*Sutera*
30.	**Nairon** Nylon	*Nailon*
31.	**Momen** Cotton	*Kapas*
32.	**Teika** Fixed price	*Harga tetap*
33.	**Mono** Things	*Barang-barang*
34.	**Chōba** Counter	*Kaunter*

35. **Uriba**   *Kaunter, Gerai*
    Counter, Stall

36. **Hokano**   *Berbeza*
    Different

37. **Akai**   *Merah*
    Red

38. **Aoi**   *Biru*
    Blue

39. **Shiroi**   *Putih*
    White

40. **Kuroi**   *Hitam*
    Black

41. **Midori**   *Hijau*
    Green

42. **Kiiro**   *Kuning*
    Yellow

43. **Momoiro**   *Merah muda*
    Pink

44. **Nezumiiro**   *Kelabu*
    Grey

45. **Murasaki**   *Ungu*
    Purple

46. **Akarui**   *Cerah*
    Light, Bright

Daijūika – (i) Hoteru (ii) Geshukuya
Pelajaran 11 – (i) Hotel (ii) Rumah Tumpangan
Lesson 11 – (i) Hotel (ii) Boarding House

1. **Irasshaimase.**
   Welcome.

   Selamat datang.

2. **Dōzo ohairi kudasai.**
   Please enter.

   Sila masuk.

3. **Watashi wa hitori heya o karitai desu.**
   I want (to rent) a single room.

   Saya hendak (sewa) sebuah bilik perseorangan.

4. **Hai, chotto matte kudasai.**
   Yes, just a moment please.

   Ya, tolong tunggu sebentar.

5. **Koko ni gokimei shite kudasai.**
   Please register here.

   Tolong daftar di sini.

6. **Hai, dōmo arigatō.**
   Yes, thank you.

   Ya, terima kasih.

7. **Koko ni o namae to go jūsho o kaite kudasai.**
   Please write your name and address here.

   Tolong tulis nama dan alamat anda di sini.

8. **Dōzo kochirae.**
   This way please.

   Tolong ikut arah ini.

9. **Kono heya ga yoroshii desu ka?**
   Is this room allright (O.K.)?

   Bilik ini sesuaikah (O.K.)?

10. **Motto yoi heya ga arimasu ka?**
    Do you have a better room?

    Adakah anda mempunyai bilik yang lebih baik?

11. **Motto ōkina heya ga arimasu ka?**
Do you have a bigger room?

Adakah anda mempunyai bilik yang lebih besar?

12. **Hai, gozaimasu.**
Yes, we have.

Ya, kami ada.

13. **Misete kudasai.**
Please show me.

Tolong tunjuk saya.

14. **Kono heya ga hitobon (ippaku) wa ikura desu ka?**
How much is this room per night?

Berapakah harganya semalam bagi bilik ini?

15. **2 (ni) man en gurai desu.**
It is about 20,000 yen.

Ianya lebih kurang 20,000 yen.

16. **Watashi wa koko ni isshukan taizai shimasu (suru) to omoimasu.**
I think I will stay here for a week.

Saya fikir saya akan menginap di sini selama seminggu.

17. **Dakkara shizukana heya ga hoshii desu.**
Therefore, I want a quiet room.

Oleh itu, saya hendak sebuah bilik yang sunyi.

18. **Sankai ni wa shizukana heya ga futatsu (nidai) arimasu.**
There are two quiet rooms on the third floor.

Ada dua buah bilik yang sunyi di tingkat ketiga.

19. **Doko no heya ga suki desu ka?**
Which room do you like?

Bilik manakah yang anda suka?

20. **Dochira ga suki desu ka, kono heya to ano heya desu ka?**
Which do you like, this or that room?

Mana satu yang anda suka, bilik inikah atau bilik itu?

21. **Obenjo wa doko desu ka?**
Where is the toilet?

Di manakah tandas?

22. **Benjo wa engawa no saki ni arimasu.**
The toilet is at the end of the verandah (porch).

Tandas itu berada di hujung serambi (porch).

23. **Nimotsu wa gozaimasu ka?**
Do you have any luggage?

Adakah anda mempunyai apa-apa barang (lugej)?

24. **Hai, takusan arimasu.**
Yes, I have much (luggage).

Ya, saya mempunyai banyak lugej.

25. **Watashi no heya ni motte kite kudasai.**
Please bring (the luggage) to my room.

Tolong bawa barang-barang itu ke bilik saya.

26. **Hai, kashikomarimashita.**
Yes, I will Sir.

Ya, saya akan tuan.

27. **Watashi wa asagohan ga irimasen.**
I don't need breakfast.

Saya tidak perlu sarapan pagi.

28. **Watashi wa mo hitotsu mofu ga hoshii desu.**
I want another blanket.

Saya hendak satu lagi selimut.

29. **Watashi wa asu no asa 5 (go) ji ni shuppatsu shimasu.**
I will leave at 5 a.m. tomorrow.

Saya akan bertolak pukul 5.00 pagi esok.

30. **Soshite, 4 (yo) ji ni okoshite kudasai.**
And, please wake me up at 4 o'clock.

Dan, tolong kejutkan saya pukul 4.00 pagi.

31. **Gogo 3 (san) ji ni kaete kimasu.**
I will return at 3 p.m.

Saya akan balik pukul 3.00 petang.

32. **Denwa o kashite kudasai.**
    May I use the phone, please.

    Tolong ... bolehkah saya guna-kan telefon.

33. **Watashi wa Marēishia e kokusai denwa o kaketai desu.**
    I want to make an overseas call to Malaysia.

    Saya hendak membuat panggilan luar negeri ke Malaysia.

34. **Koko wa geshikuya ga arimasu ka?**
    Is there a boarding house, here?

    Di sini ada rumah tumpangan-kah?

35. **Hitotsu heya ga hoshii desu.**
    I want a room.

    Saya hendak sebuah bilik.

36. **Yachin wa ikura desu ka?**
    How much is the rent?

    Berapa sewanya?

37. **Ikkagetsu wa 2 (ni) man en desu.**
    20,000 yen per month.

    20,000 yen sebulan.

38. **Hoshokin wa 3 (san) man en desu.**
    Caution money is 30,000 yen.

    Wang hemat diri ialah 30,000 yen.

39. **Denkidai to suidōryō to gasudai wa ikura desu ka?**
    How much are the electricity, water and gas rates?

    Berapakah kadar bayaran elektrik, air dan gas?

40. **Kono heya wa roku jō desu.**
    This room is 6 jō.

    Bilik ini ialah 6 jō.

1. **Bunpō**
   Grammar

   Tatabahasa

   (a) "Hoshii" is an adjective and means "want" or "desire" in English.

   "Hoshii" adalah adjektif dan bermakna "mahu" atau "meng-hendaki" dalam Bahasa Malay-sia.

(i) **Anata wa nani ga hoshii desu ka?**
What do you want?

Apa anda mahu?

(ii) **Watashi wa hitotsu heya ga hoshii desu.**
I want a room.

Saya hendak sebuah bilik.

(b) "Suki" and "kirai" are quasi-adjectives. "Suki" means "like". "Kirai" means "dislike". When they are used as quasi-adjectives, they are followed by "na" e.g. "suki na", "kirai na".

"Suki" dan "kirai" adalah quasi-adjektif. "Suki" bermakna "suka". "Kirai" bermakna "tidak suka". Apabila ia digunakan sebagai quasi-adjektif, ia diikuti oleh "na", seperti "suki na", "kirai na".

(i) **Watashi wa kono heya ga suki desu.**
I like this room.

Saya suka bilik ini.

(ii) **Watashi no ichiban suki na hito wa Taro san desu.**
My favourite (most liked) person is Mr. Taro.

Orang saya paling gemar ialah Encik Taro.

2. Dōshi
Verbs

Katakerja

Kata sekarang Present Tense ... masu	Bentuk kamus Dictionary Form ... u	Kemahuan (negatif) Desire (negative) ... takunai	Erti katakerja (Kata sekarang)
karimasu to borrow	kariru	karitakunai	meminjam
gokimei shimasu to register	gokimei suru	gokimei shitakunai	mendaftar

taizai shimasu to stay	taizai suru	taizai shitakunai	*tinggal*
shuppatsu shimasu to depart	shuppatsu suru	shuppatsu shitakunai	*bertolak*
kakemasu to hang	kakeru	kaketakunai	*menggantung*
denwa o kakemasu to telephone	denwa o kakeru	denwa o kaketakunai	*menelefon*

A. *Isikan tempat-tempat kosong dengan mana-mana perkataan yang sesuai di bawah.*

Fill in the blanks with any one of the following words.

No, ni, ga, ka, o de, to, wa, imasu, dochira, desu, kara, ji, yori

1. Tēburu _____ shita _____ nani _____ arimasu

   _____?

2. Tēburu _____ shita _____ hon _____ enpitsu

   _____ arimasu.

3. Mado _____ akete kudasai.

4. Koko _____ geshukuya _____ arimasu ka?

5. Hitotsu heya _____ karitai _____.

6. Yachin _____ ikura _____ _____?

7. Ikkagetsu _____ 2 (ni) man en _____.

8. Dochira _____ suki _____ _____, kono hon _____

   ano hon _____ _____?

9. Watashi wa Marēishia _____ kimashita.

10. Watashi wa Marēishia _____ ikitai desu.

11. Watashi _____ kaisha wa Ōsaka _____ arimasu.

12. Asa ku _____ kara, gogo san _____ made

hatarakimasu.

13. Soshite Nichiyōbi _____ yasumi desu.

14. Engawa _____ eigo _____ nan _____ iimasu _____?

15. Kono hoteru wa ano hoteru _____ takai desu.

16. Senshū _____ Nichiyōbi _____ doko _____

ikimashita _____?

17. Naze Nihon go _____ benkyo shimasu _____?

18. Naze nara suki _____.

19. Ichi nen _____ nan _____ getsu arimasu ka?

20. Ōsaka wa Shingaporu _____ ōki desu.

B. *Tukarkan ke Bahasa Jepun.*
Change into Japanese.

1. *Hotel mana yang anda suka, inikah itu?*
Which hotel do you like, this or that?

2. *Adakah anda mempunyai sebuah bilik yang sunyi?*
Do you have a quiet room?

3. *Kapal terbang itu akan bertolak pada pukul 5.00 petang hari ini.*
The aeroplane will depart at 5 p.m. today.

4. *Tolong telefon saya pagi esok.*
Please phone me tomorrow morning.

5. *Tandas itu berada di tingkat kedua.*
The toilet is on the second floor.

6. *Tandas itu berada di sebelah tepi serambi.*
The toilet is by the side of the verandah.

7. *Hari ini 2hb kah atau 3hb?*
Is today the 2nd or 3rd?

8. *Hotel itu dipanggil apa dalam Bahasa Jepun?*
How do you say hotel in Japanese?

9. *Saya bekerja dari pukul 8.00 pagi hingga 5.00 petang.*
I work from 8 a.m. to 5 p.m.

10. *Saya telah pergi ke Jepun dengan isteri saya.*
I went to Japan with my wife.

C. Fill in the blanks. *Isikan tempat-tempat kosong.*

Bentuk Kamus Dictionary Form	*Kemahuan (negatif)* Desire (negative)
taizai suru	
kariru	
hanasu	
iku	
shiru	
isogu	
kurikaesu	
shimeru	
taberu	
nomu	

Hombun
Glossary

Perbendaharaan kata

1. **Hoteru**
Hotel

Hotel

2. **Ryokan**
Japanese Inn

Rumah tumpangan Jepun

3. **Kashiya**
Vacant house

Rumah kosong

4. **Geshukuya**
Boarding house

Rumah tumpangan

5. **Genkan**
Front entrance

Pintu masuk (depan)

6. **Uchi (Ie)**
House

Rumah

7. **Heya**
Room

Bilik

8. **-Jo**
A classifier for counting tatami
(Japanese mats)

Satu 'bentuk' untuk mengira tatami (tikar Jepun)

9. **Engawa**
Verandah, Porch

Serambi, Poch

10. **Yane**
Roof

Bumbung

11. **Tenjō**
Ceiling

Siling

12. **Niwa**
Garden

Taman

13. **Hei**
Fence

Pagar

14. **Benjo, Oterai, Gofujō**
Toilet

Tandas

15. **Saki**
The end, ahead

Hujungnya, di depan

16. **Sankai**
Third floor

Tingkat tiga

17. **Hitori heya**
Single room

Bilik perseorangan

18. **Karimasu**
Borrow

Meminjam

19. **Karitai**
Want (like) to borrow

Hendak (ingin) meminjam

20. **Gokimei shimasu**
To register

Untuk mendaftar

21. **Go jūsho**
Address

Alamat

22. **Yoroshi**
Allright (O.K.)

Baik (O.K.)

23. **Yoi**
Good

Bagus (baik)

24. **Ikura?**
How much?

Berapa banyak?

25. **Gurai**
About

Kira-kira

26. **Taizai shimasu**
To stay

Untuk tinggal

27. **Taizai shitai** Want, Like to stay	*Hendak, Ingin tinggal*
28. **Nimotsu** Baggage, Luggage	*Barang-barang*
29. **Shizuka** Quiet	*Sunyi*
30. **Dochira?** Which?	*Yang mana?*
31. **Irimasu** Need	*Perlu*
32. **Irimasen** Don't need	*Tidak perlu*
33. **Mōfu** Blanket	*Selimut*
34. **Hitoban (ippaku)** One night	*Semalam (satu)*
35. **Shuppatsu** Departure	*Peninggalan*
36. **Shuppatsu shimasu** To depart	*Bertolak*
37. **Tsukimasu** To arrive	*Sampai*
38. **Kakemasu** To hang	*Untuk menggantung*
39. **Denwa o kakemasu** To telephone	*Untuk menelefon*
40. **Tatami** Japanese mats	*Tikar-tikar Jepun*

41. **Yachin**   *Sewa*
    Rental

42. **Denkidai**   *Kadar elektrik*
    Electricity rates

43. **Suidōryō**   *Kadar air*
    Water rates

44. **Gasudai**   *Kadar gas*
    Gas rates

45. **Hoshokin**   *Wang hemat diri*
    Caution money

46. **Kabe**   *Dinding*
    Wall

47. **Yuka**   *Tingkat*
    Floor

48. **To**   *Pintu*
    Door

49. **Shindai**   *Katil*
    Bed

50. **Mado**   *Tingkap*
    Window

51. **Kaidan**   *Tangga*
    Stairs

52. **Kagi**   *Kunci*
    Key

53. **Makura**   *Bantal*
    Pillow

54. **Futon**   *Tilam*
    Mattress

55. **Jutan**
Carpet

Permaidani

56. **Ka**
Mosquito

Nyamuk

57. **Kaya**
Mosquito net

Kelambu

58. **Ofuro**
A bath

Tempat mandi

59. **Furoba**
Bathroom

Bilik mandi

60. **Roka**
Corridor

Halaman, Serambi

61. **Okyaku**
A guest, Customer

Seorang tetamu, Pelanggan

62. **Kyakuma**
Guest room

Bilik tetamu

63. **Chanoma**
A living and dining room

Sebuah bilik tamu dan bilik makan

64. **Chabudai**
A low dining table

Sebuah meja makan yang rendah

65. **Daidokoro**
Kitchen

Dapur

66. **Shinshitsu**
Bedroom

Bilik tidur

67. **Tansu**
Cupboard

Almari

68. **Reizōko**
Refrigerator

Peti sejuk

124

69. **Ōsetsuma**
    Reception room

    Bilik layan tamu

70. **Yōma**
    Western-style room

    Bilik jenis barat

71. **Nihoma**
    Japanese-style room

    Bilik bergaya Jepun

Daijūnika – Yūbinkyoku
Pelajaran 12 – Pejabat Pos
Lesson 12 – Post-Office

1. **Yūbinkyoku wa doko desu ka?**
   Where is the post-office?

   Di manakah pejabat pos?

2. **Kono chikaku ni yūbinkyoku ga arimasu ka?**
   Is there a post-office near this place?

   Adakah sebuah pejabat pos berdekatan dengan tempat ini?

3. **Aruitara jūpun shika kakarimasen.**
   If you walk, it will not take more than ten minutes.

   Jika anda berjalan kaki, ia tidak akan mengambil lebih dari sepuluh minit.

4. **Takushii de nanpun kakarimasu ka?**
   How many minutes will it take by taxi?

   Berapa minitkah perjalanannya dengan teksi?

5. **Takushii deshitara sanyonpun dake kakarimasu.**
   If you take a taxi, it will only take three or four minutes.

   Jika menaiki teksi, ia akan mengambil masa tiga atau empat minit sahaja.

6. **Watashi wa kitte o kau tame ni yūbinkyoku ni(e) ikimashita.**
   I went to the post-office to buy (for the purpose of buying) stamps.

   Saya pergi ke pejabat pos untuk membeli setem.

7. **Watashi wa kawase o okuru ni yūbinkyoku ni(e) ikimashita.**
   I went to the post-office to send (for the purpose of sending) a money order.

   Saya pergi ke pejabat pos untuk mengirim wang kiriman pos.

126

8. **Kare ga kozutsumi o dasu tame ni yūbinkyoku ni(e) ikimashita.**
   He went to the post-office to send (for the purpose of sending) a parcel.

   Dia pergi ke pejabat pos untuk mengirim sebuah bungkusan.

9. **Kono tegami o kakitome ni shitai desu ga, ikura (kakarimasu) ka?**
   I want to register this letter; how much would it cost?

   Saya hendak mendaftar surat ini; berapakah bayarannya?

10. **Kono kozutsumi o Marēishia ni dashitai desu ga, ikura desu ka?**
    I want to send this parcel to Malaysia; how much would it cost?

    Saya hendak mengirim bungkusan ini ke Malaysia; berapakah bayarannya?

11. **Kakitome desu ka?**
    Is it by registered mail?

    Adakah ia dihantar secara mel berdaftar?

12. **Hai, so desu.**
    Yes, it is.

    Ya.

13. **Iie, futsū de yoroshii desu.**
    No, it will do by ordinary mail.

    Tidak, memadai secara mel biasa.

14. **Koko ni sain shite kudasai.**
    Please sign here.

    Tolong tandatangan di sini.

15. **Kakitome deshitara, ikura desu ka?**
    How much is it, if it is by registered mail?

    Berapakah bayarannya jika ia dikirim dengan mel berdaftar?

16. **Kono tegami wa kōkūbin de, ikura desu ka?**
    How much will this letter cost by air mail?

    Berapakah bayarannya surat ini secara mel udara?

17. **500 (gohyaku) en desu.**
It is 500 yen.

500 yen.

18. **Takai desu ne! Funabin de, ikura desu ka?**
Isn't it expensive? How much is it by sea mail?

Tidakkah ia mahal? Berapakah bayarannya bagi mel laut?

19. **20 (nijū) en kitte o, I (ichi) mai kudasai.**
Please give me a twenty yen stamp.

Tolong beri saya satu setem bernilai dua puluh yen.

20. **Marēishia made nannichikan kakarimasu ka?**
How many days will it take to reach Malaysia?

Berapa lamakah surat ini akan sampai ke Malaysia?

21. **Isshūkan kakarimasu.**
It takes one week.

Ia akan mengambil masa satu minggu.

22. **Isshūkan gurai kakarimasu.**
It takes about a week.

Ia akan mengambil masa kira-kira satu minggu.

23. **Denpōkyoku wa doko desu ka?**
Where is the telegraph office?

Di manakah pejabat telegraf?

24. **Yūbinkyoku no tonari ni arimasu.**
It is next to the post-office.

Ianya terletak di sebelah pejabat pos.

25. **Marēishia e shikyū denpō o uchitai desu.**
I want to send an urgent telegram to Malaysia.

Saya hendak menghantar telegram segera ke Malaysia.

26. **Itsu sukimasu ka?**
When will it reach Malaysia?

Bila ia akan sampai Malaysia?

27. **Ikura desu ka?**
How much is it?

Berapakah bayarannya?

28. **Genkin de shiharaimasu.** I will pay in cash.	*Saya akan bayar secara tunai.*
29. **Otsuri ga arimasu ka?** Do you have small change.	*Adakah anda mempunyai duit siling?*

1. Bunpō
Grammar

Tatabahasa

1. "Tame" means "purpose". It also means "for the sake of", "on behalf of", "in order to" or "for".

   "Tame" bermakna "tujuan". Ia juga bererti "oleh kerana", "bagi pihak", "supaya" atau "untuk".

   "Tame" is usually followed by the word "ni".

   "Tame" selalunya diikuti dengan perkataan "ni".

   Kitte o kau tame ni, yūbinkyoku e ikimashita. I went to the post-office to buy (for the purpose of buying) stamps.

   Saya pergi ke pejabat pos untuk membeli (bertujuan membeli) setem.

2. **Anata no tame ni kimashita.** I came because of you.

   Saya datang oleh kerana anda.

2. Dōshi
Verbs

Katakerja

Kata sekarang Present Tense	Bentuk kamus Dictionary Form	Jika (bentuk) It (form)	Jika (bentuk negatif) If (negative form)	Erti katakerja (Kata sekarang)
... masu	... u	... eba ... tara	... nakattara	
dashimasu send (a letter), take out	dasu	(daseba) dashitara if ... send	dasanakattara if ... do not send	kirim (surat), mengeluarkan

furimasu rains	furu	futtara if ... rains	furanakattara if ... does not rain	*hujan*
kashimasu lend	kasu	kashitara if ... lend	kasanakattara if ... do not lend	*meminjam*
keshimasu erase	kesu	keshitara if ... erase	kesanakattara if ... do not erase	*memadam*
nakushimasu lose	nakusu	nakushitara if ... lose	nakushinak- attara if ... do not lose	*hilang*
waraimasu laugh, smile	warau	waratara if ... smile	warawana- kattara if ... do not smile	*ketawa, senyum*
nakimasu cry	naku	naitara if ... cry	nakanakattara if ... do not cry	*menangis*
pinpon shimasu to play ping pong	pinpon suru	pinpon shitara if ... play ping pong	pinpon shina- kattara if ... not play ping pong	*bermain ping-pong*
sentaku shimasu wash clothes	sentaku suru	sentaku shitara if ... wash clothes	sentaku shinakattara if ... do not wash clothes	*basuh kain*
ki o tsukemasu be careful	ki o tsukeru	ki o tsuketara if ... careful	ki o tsukenakattara if ... not careful	*berjaga-jaga*

3. Keiyōshi
Adjectives

Adjektif

Adjektif Adjectives	Jika (bentuk) If (form) ... kereba ... kattara	Jika (bentuk negatif) If (negative form) ... kunakattara	Erti adjektif
yoi	(yokereba) yokattara	yokunakkatara	*baik*
good	if ... good	if ... not good	
warui bad	warukattara if ... bad	warukunakattara if ... not bad	*buruk*
tōi far	tōkattara if ... far	tōkunakattara if ... not far	*jauh*
akarui bright	akarukattara if ... bright	akarukanakattara if ... not bright	*cerah*
kirei beautiful	kirekattara if ... beautiful	kirekunakattara if ... not beautiful	*cantik*

4. "Deshitara" "(Dattara)"
The "if" form of "desu" is
"deshitara".

Bentuk 'jika' bagi "desu" ialah "deshitara".

A. *Terjemahkan dalam bahasa Jepun.*
Change into Japanese.

1. *Di manakah pejabat pos?*
Where is the post-office?

2. *Tolong berikan dua puluh setem yang bernilai sepuluh yen.*
20 ten yen stamps, please.

3. *Jika saya mengirim poskad ini hari ini, bilakah ia akan sampai di Tokyo?*
If I send this postcard today, when will it arrive in Tokyo?

4. *Kami pergi ke pejabat pos untuk mengirim (bertujuan mengirim) wang kiriman pos.*
We went to the post-office to send (for the purpose of sending) a money order.

5. *Jika anda berjalan kaki ke pejabat pos ia tidak akan mengambil lebih dari tiga minit.*
If you walk to the post-office it will not take more than three minutes.

6. *Jika saya adalah anda, saya tidak akan bekerja di sini.*
If I were you, I will not work here.

7. *Jika ia (perempuan) cantik, dia (lelaki) akan mengahwininya.*
If she is beautiful, he will marry her.

8. *Jika anda tidak pergi dari sini, saya akan menangis.*
If you do not go away from here I will cry.

9. *Jika cuaca elok, saya hendak berjalan ke pejabat pos.*
If the weather is good, I want to walk to the post-office.

B. *Susun kembali ayat-ayat di bawah.*
Rearrange the following sentences.

1. doko wa ka yūbinkyoku desu.

2. desu dashitai desu kono ka? ikura o ga tegami.

3. kudasai tegami o shite kono kakitome ni.

4. kudasai koko shite ni sain.

5. tōi wa koko yūbinkyoku desu kara ka?

6. ittara wa Tōkyō anata katte o ni ka kudasaimasen hagaki.

7. Yasumi wa ka Tōkyō ashita ni deshitara ikimashyoo.

132

C. Fill in the blanks.   *Isikan tempat-tempat kosong.*

Perkataan Words	*Jika (bentuk)* If (form)	*Jika (bentuk negatif)* If (Negative form)
tabemasu		
okurimasu		
yasumimasu		
yomimasu		
naraimasu		
unten shimasu		
desu		
warui		
yoi		
toi		

Hombun
Glossary

Perbendaharaan kata

1. **Yūbinkyoku**
   Post-office

   Pejabat Pos

2. **Kawase**
   Money order

   Wang kiriman pos

3. **Kozutsumi**
   Parcel, Parcel post

   Bungkusan, Bungkusan pos

4. **Kakitome**
   Registered

   Berdaftar

5. **Sokutatsu** *Ekspres*
   Express

6. **Kitte** *Setem*
   Stamps

7. **Shika** *Sahaja*
   Only

8. **Posuto** *Sebuah peti mel, Peti surat*
   A mail box, A post box

9. **Tonari** *Rumah sebelah*
   Next door

10. **Funabin** *Mel-laut*
    Sea-mail

11. **Futsū** *Biasa*
    Usual, Ordinary

12. **Genkin** *Tunai*
    Cash

13. **Yūbin butsu** *Mel*
    Mail

14. **Tegami** *Surat*
    Letter

15. **Jushinin** *Penerima surat*
    Addressee

16. **Hasshinin** *Pengirim*
    Sender

17. **Hagaki** *Poskad*
    Post-card

18. **Denpō** *Telegeram*
    Telegram

19. **Shikyū denpō**
    Urgent telegram

    Telegeram serta-merta

20. **Sain**
    Sign (name)

    Tandatangani (nama)

21. **Dashimasu**
    To send (letter), To take out

    Untuk mengirim (surat),
    Mengeluarkan

22. **Denpō kyoku**
    Telegraph office

    Pejabat telegeraf

23. **Otsuri**
    Small change

    Pertukaran duit siling

24. **Unten shimasu**
    To drive

    Memandu

Daijūsanka - Byōki
Pelajaran 13 - Penyakit
Lesson 13 - Sickness

1. **Dō shita no desu ka?**
   What is the matter with you?

   Apa hal dengan kamu?

2. **Dōnasai mashita ka?**
   What is wrong with you?

   Apa kena dengan dirimu?

3. **Doko ga warui desu ka?**
   What ails you?

   Apa yang menyusahkan kamu?

4. **Watashi wa byōki desu.**
   I am sick.

   Saya sakit.

5. **Kibun ga warui desu ka?**
   Are you feeling uncomfortable?

   Adakah anda rasa tidak selesa?

6. **Atama ga itai desu.**
   Zutsū ga shimasu.
   I have a headache.

   Saya sakit kepala.

7. **Onaka ga itai desu.**
   Fukutsu ga shimasu.
   I have a stomachache.

   Saya sakit perut.

8. **Itsu kara itai desu ka?**
   Since when was the pain?

   Sejak bila sakitnya?

9. **Yūbe kara desu.**
   From last night.

   Sejak semalam.

10. **Netsu ga arimasu ka?**
    Do you have a fever?

    Anda demamkah?

11. **Hai, shukoshi arimasu.**
    Yes, I have a slight fever.

    Ya, saya demam sedikit.

12. **Netsu ga nando arimasu ka?**
What is your temperature?

Berapakah suhu badan kamu?

13. **(Kashi) hyaku ichi do arimasu.**
101°F degrees.

101 darjah Fahrenheit.

14. **Seki ga arimasu ka?**
Do you have a cough?

Anda batukkah?

15. **Hai, seki ga chotto (shukoshi) arimasu.**
Yes, I have a slight cough.

Ya, saya batuk sedikit.

16. **Kaze ga hikimashita ka?**
Have you caught a cold?

Anda selsemakah?

17. **Ima wa nemutai desu ka?**
Are you sleepy now?

Adakah anda mengantuk sekarang?

18. **Hai, nemutai desu.**
Yes, I am sleepy.

Ya, saya mengantuk.

19. **Dōzo yasunde kudasai.**
Please rest.

Sila rehat.

20. **Shoka no mondai ga arimasu ka?**
Do you have problems with your digestion?

Adakah anda mempunyai masalah dengan penghadaman kamu?

21. **Anata wa hatarakusugi desu.**
You work too hard.

Anda bekerja berlebihan.

22. **Kono kusuri o yonde kudasai.**
Please take (drink) this medicine.

Tolong ambil (minum) ubat ini.

23. **Kusuriya ga doko ni arimasu ka?**
Where is the pharmacy?

Di manakah kedai ubat?

24. **Kusuriya ga doko ni imasu ka?**
    Where is the chemist?

    Di manakah pakar ubat?

25. **Kusuriya kara kusuri o katte kudasai.**
    Please buy the medicine from the chemist.

    Tolong beli ubat itu dari pakar ubat.

26. **Watashi wa hidoi byōki de nyūin shimashita.**
    I was hospitalized due to a serious illness.

    Saya telah dimasukkan ke hospital disebabkan oleh satu penyakit yang serius.

27. **Kinō wa taiin shimashita.**
    I was discharged (from hospital) yesterday.

    Saya telah dibenarkan pulang (dari hospital) kelmarin.

28. **Naze yasumimashita ka?**
    Why were you absent?

    Mengapa kamu tidak hadir?

29. **Byōki kara deshita.**
    Because I was ill.

    Sebab saya sakit.

30. **Taro san wa gakkō ni kimashita ka?**
    Did Mr. Taro come to school?

    Sudahkah En. Taro datang ke sekolah?

31. **Iie, yasumi desu.**
    No, he is absent.

    Tidak, dia tidak hadir.

32. **Dōshite desu ka?**
    Why?

    Mengapa?

33. **Naze nara karada ga yowai desu.**
    Because he (his body) is weak.

    Kerana dia (badannya) lemah.

34. **Karada ga yowaku narimashita.**
    My body has become weak.

    Badan saya semakin lemah.

138

35. **Kare wa byōki ni narimashita.**
    He is ill.

Dia tidak sihat.

36. **Tabako wa takusan suimasu ka?**
    Do you smoke many cigarettes?
    (Do you smoke heavily?)

Adakah anda banyak merokok?

37. **Ichinichi wa nanpon suimasu ka?**
    How many sticks do you smoke per day?

Berapa batang rokokkah anda merokok setiap hari?

38. **50 (gojū) pon desu.**
    50 sticks.

50 batang rokok.

39. **Tabako wa takusan suwanaide kudasai.**
    Please don't smoke heavily.

Tolong jangan merokok banyak-banyak.

40. **(Anata wa) byōki kara, yoku yasumanakereba narimasen.**
    Since you are ill, you must rest well.

Oleh kerana anda sakit, anda mesti berehat betul-betul.

41. **Kono kusuri o nomanakereba narimasen.**
    You must take (drink) this medicine.

Anda mesti makan (minum) ubat ini.

Bunpō
Grammar

Tatabahasa

1. (a) "... ni Narimasu" means "to become". It also means "turn into", "change into" etc. "Narimasu" usually takes "ni" when it follows a noun.

"... ni Narimasu" bermakna "untuk menjadi". Ia juga bermakna "belok ke dalam"; "tukarkan ke dalam" dsb. "Narimasu" selalunya mengambil "ni" apabila ia mengikuti nama.

(i) **Ichi to ni de ikutsu ni**   *Satu dan dua menjadi apa?*
    narimasu ka?
    One and two becomes
    what?

(ii) **San ni narimasu.**   *Ia menjadi tiga.*
     It becomes three.

(iii) **Watashi wa sensei ni**   *Saya hendak/suka menjadi*
      naritai desu.   *seorang guru.*
      I would like to become
      a teacher.

(b) "Narimasu" can also be   *Boleh juga digunakan dengan*
    used with an adjective e.g.   *adjektif iaitu menjadi cantik.*
    kireku narimasu.

    (i) **Kanojo wa okane-**   *Dia menjadi kaya.*
        mochi ni narimashita.
        She became rich.

2. Dōshi
Verbs

Katakerja

Kata sekarang Present Tense ... masu	*Bentuk kamus* Dictionary Form ... u	*Bentuk suruhan* *Negatif (Halus)* Please Don't (negative) ... naide kudasai	*Harus (mesti)* "Must" form ... nakereba narimasen	*Erti katakerja* (*Kata sekarang*)
nemasu sleep	**neru**	**nenaide kudasai**	**nenakereba narimasen**	*tidur*
suimasu to smoke	**su**	**suwanaide kudasai**	**suwanakereba narimasen**	*menghisap*
bunkai shimasu disassemble	**bunkai suru**	**bunkai shinaide kudasai**	**bunkai shinakereba narimasen**	*meleraikan*
shinpai shimasu to worry	**shinpai suru**	**shinpai shinaide kudasai**	**shinpai shinakereba narimasen**	*khuatir*
chōsetsu shimasu to adjust	**chōsetsu suru**	**chōsetsu shinaide kudasai**	**chōsetsu shinakereba narimasen**	*menyesuaikan*
jisshu shimasu to have practical training	**jisshu suru**	**jisshu shinaide kudasai**	**jisshu shinakereba narimasen**	*latihan praktikal*
shuri shimasu to repair	**shūri suru**	**shūri shinaide kudasai**	**shūri shinakereba narimasen**	*perbaiki*
sōsa shimasu to operate (machines etc.)	**sōsa suru**	**sosa shinaide kudasai**	**sosa shinakereba narimasen**	*menjalankan*

A. Translate into Japanese.

Terjemahkan ke bahasa Jepun.

Doctor:	What is wrong with you?	*Apa yang tidak kena dengan kamu?*
Patient:	I have caught a cold. I also have a headache.	*Saya dihinggapi selsema. Saya juga mengalami sakit kepala.*
Doctor:	You have a slight fever. Did you have a fever, yesterday?	*Kamu kurang sihat. Kamu demamkah semalam?*
Patient:	I don't know.	*Saya tidak tahu.*
Doctor:	Do you feel faint?	*Adakah anda rasa pening?*
Patient:	Yes, I feel faint.	*Ya, saya rasa pening.*
Doctor to Nurse:	Please bring the thermometer.	*Tolong bawa jangkasuhu.*
Patient:	What is the temperature?	*Berapakah suhu badan?*
Doctor:	37 degrees Centigrade.	*37 darjah Centigrade.*
Patient:	Since I am feeling very uncomfortable, could you please give me medicine?	*Oleh kerana saya merasa tidak selesa, bolehkah tuan berikan saya ubat?*
Doctor:	Please (take) this medicine.	*Tolong minum (ambil) ubat ini.*
Patient:	Thank you.	*Terima kasih.*
Doctor:	Take care of yourself.	*Jagalah diri kamu.*

B. *Tukarkan yang berikut ke bahasa Jepun.*
   Change the following into Japanese.

   1. Please don't smoke.   *Tolong jangan merokok.*

142

2. Please don't come to my house tomorrow.

Tolong jangan datang ke rumah saya esok.

3. If you don't drink this medicine, you will become more ill.

Jika anda tidak minum ubat ini, demam anda akan melarat.

4. You must work very hard.

Anda mesti bekerja kuat.

5. You must pass this examination.

Anda mesti lulus peperiksaan ini.

C. *Buatkan ayat dengan yang berikut:*
   Make sentences with the following:

(a) **tabenaide kudasai**

(b) **ikanaide kudasai**

(c) **kekkon shinaide kudasai**

(d) **uranaide kudasai**

(e) **saboranaide kudasai**

(f) **yomanakereba narimasen**

(g) **ikanakereba narimasen**

(h) **konakereba narimasen**

(i) **hatarakanakereba narimasen**

(j) **sōji shinakereba narimasen**

(k) **shūri shinakereba narimasen**

(l) **benkyō shinakereba narimasen**

Hombun Glossary	*Perbendaharaan kata*
1. **Karada** Body	*Tubuh badan*
2. **Kakato** Ankle	*Pergelangan kaki*
3. **Oya yubi** Thumb	*Ibu jari*
4. **Kaze** Flu	*Selsema*
5. **Seki** Cough	*Batuk*
6. **Kega** Injuries	*Kecederaan*
7. **Kega o shimasu** To be injured	*Tercedera*
8. **Kizu** Wound	*Luka*
9. **Byōki** Sick	*Sakit*
10. **Byōnin, Kanja** Patient	*Pesakit*
11. **Nyūin** Hospitalized	*Dimasukkan ke hospital*
12. **Taiin** Discharged (from hospital)	*Dibenarkan keluar (dari hospital)*
13. **Nyushin** Pregnant	*Hamil*

14. **Nodo ga kawakimasu** *Dahaga*
Thirsty

15. **Onaka ga sukimasu** *Lapar*
Hungry

16. **Hikimasu** *Di hinggapi, mithalnya selsema*
To catch e.g. a cold

17. **Taishita** *Serius*
Serious

18. **Shinpai** *Risau*
Worries

19. **Shinpai shimasu** *Risau*
To worry

20. **Bunkai shimasu** *Meleraikan*
Disassemble

21. **Chōsetsu shimasu** *Menyesuaikan*
To adjust

22. **Jisshu shimasu** *Mempunyai latihan praktikal*
To have practical training

23. **Shūri shimasu** *Untuk membaiki*
To repair

24. **Sōsa shimasu** *Menjalankan*
To operate (machines)

25. **Chūsha** *Suntikan*
Injection

26. **Shinsatsu shitsu** *Klinik*
Clinic

27. **Kusuri** *Ubat*
Medicine

28. **Shujutsu** *Pembedahan*
Surgical operation

29. **Netsu** *Demam*
Fever

30. **Seki** *Batuk*
Cough

31. **Suimasu** *Menghisap*
To smoke

32. **Kanbo** *Demam selsema*
Influenza

33. **Benpi** *Sembelit*
Constipation

34. **Geri** *Ceret-beret*
Diarrhoea

35. **Hidoi** *Serius*
Serious

36. **Mekura** *Orang buta*
Blind person

37. **Tsumbo** *Orang pekak*
Deaf, Deaf person

Daijūyonka - Kōtsū
Pelajaran 14 – Lalu lintas
Lesson 14 – Traffic

1. **Eki wa doko desu ka?**
   Where is the railway station?

   Di manakah stesyen keretapi itu?

2. **Masugu itte, migi ni magatte kudasai.**
   Go straight and please turn to the right.

   Pergi jalan terus dan tolong belok ke kanan.

3. **Tsugi no kado o hidari e magatte kudasai.**
   Please turn at the next corner.

   Tolong belok di selekoh yang seterusnya.

4. **Sanban me (mitsu me) no kado o migi ni magatte kudasai.**
   Please turn right at the third corner.

   Tolong belok kanan di selekoh yang ketiga.

5. **Anata wa hikōki o notta koto ga arimasu ka?**
   Have you ever boarded a plane?

   Pernahkah anda menaiki kapal terbang?

6. **Hai, notta koto ga arimasu.**
   Yes, I have boarded a plane.

   Ya, saya pernah menaiki kapal terbang.

7. **Iie, notta koto ga arimasen.**
   No, I have never boarded a plane.

   Tidak, saya tidak pernah menaiki kapal terbang.

8. **Shinkansen o notta koto ga arimasu ka?**
   Have you ever boarded the Shinkansen?

   Pernahkah anda menaiki "shinkansen"?

9. **Shinkansen wa Tōkyō kara Hakata made hashirimasu.**
Shinkansen runs from Tokyo to Hakata.

"Shinkansen" melalui Tokyo ke Hakata.

10. **Hikari to Kodama ga Nagoya ni tōrimasu ka?**
Does the Hikari and Kodama pass (through) Nagoya?

Adakah Hikari dan Kodama melalui (melintasi) Nagoya?

11. **Kippu wa doko de kaimasu ka?**
Where do I buy tickets?

Di manakah saya boleh membeli tiket?

12. **Ano madoguchi de katte kudasai.**
Please buy at that window (over there).

Tolong beli melalui tingkap (di sana).

13. **Hakata iki no kippu o kudasai.**
Give me a ticket to Hakata, please.

Tolong berikan saya satu tiket ke Hakata.

14. **Hikari ga nanji ni demasu ka?**
What time does the Hikkari leave?

Pukul berapakah Hikkari bertolak?

15. **Hachi ji ni deru hazu desu.**
It is supposed to leave at 8 o'clock.

Ia sepatutnya bertolak pada pukul 8.00.

16. **Tsugi no densha wa goban no hōmu kara notte kudasai.**
Please board the next train from platform 5.

Tolong naik keretapi yang seterusnya dari platform 5.

17. **Kodama ni shokudōsha ga arimasu ka?**
Is there a "dining car" in the Kodama?

Adakah gerabak makan di dalam Kodama?

18. **Kotsū jiko ga mita koto ga arimasu ka?**
Have you (ever) seen a traffic accident?

Pernahkah anda melihat kemalangan jalan raya?

19. **Kinō wa kōtsū jiko ga mimashita.**
I saw a traffic accident yesterday.

Saya melihat satu kemalangan jalan raya kelmarin.

20. **Jidōsha wa jitensha o butsukarimashita.**
A car hit a bicycle.

Sebuah kereta melanggar sebuah basikal.

21. **Hitori norinin ga kega o shimashita.**
A passenger was injured.

Seorang penumpang telah cedera.

22. **Kinkyūsha ga suite, keganin o byōin ni hakobimashita.**
An ambulance arrived and took the injured person to the hospital.

Sebuah ambulan tiba dan menghantar (membawa) orang yang cedera itu ke hospital.

23. **Gemba no chikaku wa kōban ga arimasen deshita.**
There was no police box near the scene (of the accident).

Di situ tidak terdapat pondok polis berhampiran dengan tempat kejadian.

24. **Unten suru koto ga dekimasu ka?**
Can you drive?

Bolehkah anda memandu?

25. **Anata wa fune de koraremashita ka?**
Did you come by ship?

Anda datang dengan kapalkah?

26. **Hai, fune de kimashita.**
Yes, I came by ship.

Ya, saya datang dengan kapal.

27. **Kono fune ga Ōsaka ni ikimasu ka?**
Is this ship going to Osaka?

Kapal ini pergi ke Osakakah?

28. **Ōsaka wa mada desu ka?**
Have we reached Osaka yet?

Sudahkah kita sampai ke Osaka?

29. **Ōsaka ni gogo 3 (san)ji ni tsuku hazu desu.**
It is supposed to arrive at Osaka at 3 p.m.

Ia sepatutnya tiba di Osaka pada 3 petang.

30. **Mō sūgu desu.**
Very soon.

Tidak lama lagi.

Bunpō
Grammar

Tatabahasa

1. (a) "Hazu" means "supposed to".

"Hazu" bermakna "sepatutnya".

   (i) **Kinō wa Shingaporu e iku hazu deshita.**
I was supposed to go to Singapore yesterday.

Saya sepatutnya pergi ke Singapura kelmarin.

2. **Dōshi**
Verbs

Katakerja

Kala sekarang Present Tense	Bentuk kamus Dictionary Form	Pengalaman lampau Past Experience	Erti katakerja (Kata sekarang)
... masu	... u	... ta koto ga arimasu	
norimasu to board	noru	notta koto ga arimasu	menaiki
tomemasu to stop	tomeru	tometa koto ga arimasu	berhenti

kaimono shimasu to do shopping	kaimono suru	kaimono shita koto ga arimasu	*membeli-belah*
shokuji shimasu to take meals, dine	shokuji suru	shokuji shita koto ga arimasu	*makan*
kenka shimasu to quarrel	kenka suru	kenka shita koto ga arimasu	*bergaduh*

A. Tukarkan ke Bahasa Jepun.
Change into Japanese.

1. Next year I want to go to Tokyo.

Tahun depan saya hendak pergi ke Tokyo.

2. How will you go?

Bagaimana kamu akan pergi?

3. Please give me a ticket for Tokyo.

Tolong berikan saya satu tiket ke Tokyo.

4. Please give a ticket for the 1st of August.

Tolong berikan satu tiket bagi 1hb Ogos.

5. What is the next station?

Apakah stesyen seterusnya?

6. Have you been to Ginza by the subway?

Pernahkah anda pergi ke Ginza dengan keretapi bawah tanah?

7. Please call a taxi.

Tolong panggil sebuah teksi.

8. Does this train stop at Ōsaka?

Adakah keretapi ini berhenti di Osaka?

9. Please turn to the right.

Tolong belok ke kanan.

10. I want to take a plane.

Saya hendak menaiki kapal terbang.

B. *Berikan perkataan berlawan perkataan-perkataan yang tersebut.*
Give the opposite of the following words.

(i) **Ue**   (xi) **Suwarimasu**

(ii) **Ōkii**   (xii) **Shiroi**

(iii) **Chotto**   (xiii) **Hairimasu**

(iv) **Okanemochi**   (xiv) **Okurimasu**

(v) **Shuppatsu shimasu**   (xv) **Yasui**

(vi) **Migi**   (xvi) **Atsui**

(vii) **Norimasu**   (xvii) **Suzushi**

(viii) **Kaimasu**   (xviii) **Arukimasu**

(ix) **Nemasu**   (xix) **Danyū**

(x) **Ikimasu**   (xx) **Akemasu**

C. *Buatkan ayat dengan perkataan-perkataan yang berikut:*
Make sentences with the following:

(1) **Notta koto ga arimasu**

(2) **Kaimono shita koto ga arimasu**

(3) **Itta koto ga arimasu ka?**

(4) **Tabeta koto ga arimasen**

(5) **Kenka shita koto ga arimasu ka?**

(6) **Shōji shita koto ga arimasu ka?**

(7) **Hazu**

(8) **Sūgu**

(9) **Noritai**

(10) **Ikitai**

Hombun Glossary	*Perbendaharaan Kata*
1. **Kōtsū** Traffic	*Lalulintas*
2. **Jiko** Accident	*Kemalangan*
3. **Kyūko** Express	*Ekspres*
4. **Kisha** Train	*Keretapi*
5. **Densha** Electric train	*Keretapi letrik*
6. **Chikatetsu** Subway	*Keretapi bawah tanah*
7. **Shindaisha** Sleeping car (in a train)	*Gerabak untuk tidur* *(dalam keretapi)*
8. **Eki** Station	*Stesyen*
9. **Fune** Ship	*Kapal*
10. **Kyakusen** Passenger ship	*Kapal penumpang*
11. **Kamotsuen** Cargo ship	*Kapal kargo*

12. **Kippu** Ticket		*Tiket*
13. **Kado** Corner, Bend		*Selekoh*
14. **Migi** Right		*Kanan*
15. **Hidari** Left		*Kiri*
16. **Minami** South		*Selatan*
17. **Kita** North		*Utara*
18. **Higashi** East		*Timur*
19. **Nishi** West		*Barat*
20. **Minato** Harbour		*Pelabuhan*
21. **Hikōjō** Airport		*Lapangan terbang*
22. **Senchō** Captain (ship)		*Kapten (kapal)*
23. **Butsukarimasu** To knock (against)		*Dilanggar (bertentangan)*
24. **Kega** Injuries		*Kecederaan*

Daijūgoka – Shūshoku
Pelajaran 15 – Pekerjaan
Lesson 15 – Employment

1. **Anata wa ima doko de hataraiteimasu ka?**
   Where are you working now?

   Di manakah anda bekerja sekarang?

2. **Matsushita de hataraiteimasu.**
   I am working at Matsushita.

   Saya bekerja di Matsushita.

3. **Kono kaisha de nannenkan hataraiteimasu ka?**
   How many years have you been working in this company?

   Sudah berapa tahunkah anda bekerja di syarikat ini?

4. **8 (hachi) nenkan desu.**
   8 years.

   Sudah 8 tahun.

5. **Anata wa keiken ga arimasu ka?**
   Do you have experience?

   Adakah anda mempunyai pengalaman?

6. **Nannen no keiken ga arimasu ka?**
   How many years of experience do you have?

   Berapa tahunkah pengalaman yang anda miliki?

7. **15 (jūgo) nen no keiken ga arimasu.**
   15 years of experience.

   Pengalaman selama 15 tahun.

8. **Kōjō de hataraku koto ga dekimasu ka?**
   Can you work at the factory?

   Bolehkah anda bekerja di kilang?

9. **Mensetsu ni ikimashita ka?**
   Did you go for the interview?

   Adakah anda menghadiri temuduga itu?

10. **Mensetsu nashi de, kaisha e hairu koto ga dekimasen.**
Without an interview, one cannot work for the company.

Tanpa temuduga seseorang itu tidak boleh bekerja untuk syarikat tersebut.

11. **Doko no daigaku o sotsugyō shimashita ka?**
From which university did you graduate?

Anda mempunyai kelulusan dari universiti mana?

12. **Mareiya daigaku o sotsugyō shimashita.**
I graduated from the University of Malaya.

Saya berkelulusan dari Universiti Malaya.

13. **Senmon wa nan desu ka?**
What is your field of specialization?

Apakah bidang pengkhususan (latihan) anda?

14. **Kyūryō wa ikura hoshii desu ka?**
How much salary do you expect?

Berapa banyakkah gaji yang anda kehendaki?

15. **500 (gohyaku) doru ga hoshii desu.**
I expect $500.

Saya mahu $500.

16. **Saisho wa 350 (sambyaku gojū) doru ga dashimasu.**
(The Company) will give you $350 at the beginning.

Pada permulaannya syarikat ini akan membayar sebanyak $350 kepada anda.

17. **Ichinen go gojū doru ga neageshimasu.**
(The company) will give a $50 increment after one year.

Syarikat ini akan membayar kenaikan sebanyak $50 selepas setahun.

18. **Bōnasu ga arimasu ka?**
Is there a bonus?

Ada bonuskah?

19. **Kaisha wa kōtsū hi ga dashimasu.**
The company gives travelling allowance.

Syarikat ini akan memberi elaun perjalanan.

20. **Hokano teate ga arimasu ka?**
Are there any other allowances?

Adakah apa-apa elaun yang lain?

21. **Kono kaisha de jugyōin wa nannin imasu ka?**
How many factory workers are there in this company?

Berapa ramaikah pekerja kilang yang ada di syarikat ini?

22. **Jimuin ga nannin imasu ka?**
How many office workers are there?

Berapa ramaikah pekerja pejabat yang ada?

23. **Shain ga nannin imasu ka?**
How many company employees are there?

Berapa ramaikah pekerja syarikat ini?

24. **Ichinen ni kyūka ga nannichikan desu ka?**
How many days of annual leave do you give in a year?

Berapa harikah cuti tahunan yang anda beri dalam setahun?

25. **3 (sanshū) kan desu.**
Three weeks.

Tiga minggu.

26. **Ishūkan ni nannichikan wa hatarakimasu ka?**
How many days do you work in a week?

Berapa harikah anda bekerja dalam seminggu?

27. **Itsukakan ga hatarakimasu.**
5 days.

Lima hari.

28. **Zangyō (chōka kimu) ga arimasu ka?**
Is there any overtime?

Ada kerja lebih masakah?

29. **Kaisha wa nanji kara hajimemasu ka?**
What time does the company start?

Dari pukul berapakah syarikat ini dibuka?

30. **Raishū wa kaisha o yametai desu.**
I want to resign from the company as of next week.

Saya mahu meletakkan jawatan dari syarikat ini mulai minggu depan.

31. **Kyūryobi wa tsuki no saigo no hi desu.**
Payday is the last day of the month.

Hari pembayaran gaji adalah hari terakhir dalam satu-satu bulan itu.

32. **Ishūkan no kyūka wa toru koto ga dekimasu ka?**
Can I take one week's leave?

Bolehkah saya mengambil cuti untuk seminggu?

33. **Kyuka ni doko ka ikitai desu ka?**
Where do you want to go for your holidays?

Ke manakah anda mahu pergi semasa cuti?

34. **Ima no tokoro wa yotei ga arimasen.**
I do not have any plans at present.

Pada masa ini saya belum mempunyai apa-apa rancangan.

35. **Watashi wa ryoko ni kyōmi ga arimasen.**
I am not interested in travelling.

Saya tidak berminat dengan pelancongan.

36. **Gakkō ni modoritai desu.**
I want to return (go back) to school.

Saya ingin bersekolah semula.

37. **Kyūryō wa yasukutemo, hatarakitai desu.**
Even if the salary is low, I want/ like to work.

Walaupun gajinya rendah, saya mahu/suka bekerja.

38. **Yoku hataraitemo, bōnasu ga moraimasen deshita.**
Even though I worked hard, I did not receive any bonus.

Walaupun saya bekerja kuat, saya tidak menerima apa-apa bonus.

1. Dōshi
Katakerja
Verbs

Kata sekarang	Bentuk walaupun	Bentuk walaupun	Bentuk kemungkinan (bolehkah)	Erti katakerja (Kata sekarang)
Present Tense ... masu	Dictionary Form ... u	Even if (form) ... te mo ... de mo	Can you (Potential form) ... u koto ga dekimasu	
moraimasu receive	**morau**	**morate mo** even if ... receive	**morau koto ga dekimasu** can ... receive	*menerima*
sotsugyō shimasu to graduate	**sotsugyō suru**	**sotsugyō shite mo** even if ... graduate	**sotsugyō suru koto ga dekimasu** can ... graduate	*untuk mendapat ijazah*
nirimasu to cook, boil	**niru**	**nite mo** even if ... cook, boil	**niru koto ga dekimasu** can ... cook, boil	*memasak, mendidih*
nokku shimasu to knock	**nokku suru**	**nokku shite mo** even if ... knock	**nokku suru koto ga dekimasu** can ... knock	*ketuk*
setsumei shimasu to explain	**setsumei suru**	**sotsugyō shite mo** even if ... explain	**setsumei suru koto ga dekimasu** can ... explain	*untuk menyelaskan*
shitsumon shimasu to question	**shitsumon suru**	**shitsumon shite mo** even if ... question	**shitsumon suru koto ga dekimasu** can ... question	*untuk menyoal*

umaremasu to be born	**umareru**	**umarete mo** even if ... born	**umareru koto ga dekimasu** can ... born	*dilahirkan*
yamemasu to stop, quit, retire	**yameru**	**yamete mo** even if ... stop	**yameru koto ga dekimasu** can ... stop	*berhenti,* *meninggalkan, bersara*
shirabemasu to check, investigate	**shiraberu**	**shirabete mo** even if ... investigate	**shiraberu koto ga dekimasu** can ... investigate	*memeriksa, menyiasat*
agemasu give	**ageru**	**agete mo** even if ... give	**ageru koto ga dekimasu** can ... give	*beri*

2. Keiyōshi
Adjective

Adjektif

Adjektif Adjectives	*Bentuk walaupun* Even if ...	*Erti Adjektif*
katai hard	**katakutemo** even if ... hard	*keras*
yawarakai soft	**yawarakakutemo** even if ... soft	*lembut*
atarashii new	**atarashikutemo** even if ... new	*baru*
furui old	**furukutemo** even if ... old	*lama*
osoi slow	**osokutemo** even if ... slow	*perlahan*
hayai early, fast	**hayakutemo** even if ... early	*awal, cepat*
hiroi wide	**hirokutemo** even if ... wide	*lebar, luas*
semai narrow	**semakutemo** even if ... narrow	*sempit*
omoshiroi interesting	**omoshirokutemo** even if ... interesting	*menarik*
tsumaranai dull	**tsumaranakutemo** even if ... dull	*bosan*
oishii delicious	**oishikutemo** even if ... delicious	*sedap, lazat*

mazui tasteless	mazukutemo even if … tasteless	*tiada rasa*
muzukashii difficult	muzukashikutemo even if … difficult	*sukar*
yasashii easy, gentle	yasashikutemo even if … easy	*mudah, lembut*
amai sweet	amakutemo even if … sweet	*manis*

A. *Tukarkan ke dalam Bahasa Jepun.*
   Change into Japanese.

1. *Semalam saya pergi temuduga.*
   Yesterday I went for an interview.

2. *Anda lulus dari universiti mana?*
   Which university did you graduate from?

3. *Setelah lulus dari universiti apakah yang anda buat?*
   After graduating what did you do?

4. *Saya menjadi guru Bahasa Jepun selama tiga tahun.*
   I became a Japanese language teacher for three years.

5. *Bolehkah anda mula bekerja esok?*
   Can you start work tomorrow?

6. *Walaupun anda datang ke rumah saya ianya tidak berguna.*
   Even if you come to my house it is useless.

7. *Walaupun makanan itu mahal, rasanya lazat.*
   Even though the meal was expensive, it was very delicious.

8. *Bolehkah saya menerima gaji pada hari ini?*
   Can I receive my pay today?

B. *Buat ayat dengan menggunakan perkataan-perkataan berikut:*
Make sentences with the following words:

(1) **itte mo**

(2) **furukute mo**

(3) **yasukute mo**

(4) **nonde mo**

(5) **yonde mo**

(6) **sōji shite mo**

(7) **yokute mo**

(8) **amakute mo**

(9) **semakute mo**

(10) **akarukute mo**

(11) **yowakute mo**

(12) **kangaete mo**

(13) **irete mo**

(14) **wasurete mo**

(15) **taberu koto ga dekimasen**

(16) **iku koto ga dekimasen**

(17) **yomu koto ga dekimasen**

(18) **kaku koto ga dekimasen**

(19) **miru koto ga dekimasen**

164

(20) **tabete kara**

C. *Isikan tempat-tempat kosong.*
   Fill in the blanks.

Perkataan Words	Bolehkah anda Can you	(Bentuk) walaupun Even if (form)
sawarimasu		
tsukaimasu		
ugokimasu		
nugimasu		
urimasu		
tachimasu		
oyogimasu		
tabemasu		

Hombun
Glossary

Perbendaharaan Kata

1. **Shūshoku**
   Employment

   Pekerjaan

2. **Shitsugyo**
   Unemployment

   Pengangguran

3. **Shigoto**
   Work (noun)

   Pekerjaan

4. **Keiken**
   Experience

   Pengalaman

5. **Sotsugyō shimasu**
   Graduate

   Berijazah

6. **Sotsugyō shiki**
   Graduation ceremony

   Upacara penyampaian ijazah

7. **Kyūryō**
   Salary

   Gaji

8. **Zangyō** — *Lebih masa*
Overtime

9. **Taishoku** — *Persaraan*
Retirement

10. **Bōnasu** — *Bonus*
Bonus

11. **Teate** — *Elaun*
Allowances

12. **Kyūka** — *Cuti*
Holiday

13. **Shain** — *Pekerja syarikat*
Company employees

14. **Jimuin** — *Pekerja pejabat*
Office worker

15. **Jimusho, Jimushitsu** — *Pejabat*
Office

16. **Jugyōin** — *Pekerja kilang*
Factory workers

17. **Kōjō** — *Kilang*
Factory

18. **Rōdō** — *Buruh*
Labour

19. **Rōdō kumiai** — *Kesatuan buruh*
Labour unions

20. **Ryō** — *Asrama*
Dormitory

21. **Shachō** — *Presiden (Syarikat)*
President (of a company)

22. **Buchō**　　　　　　　　*Pengurus*
    Manager

23. **Kachō**　　　　　　　　*Ketua bahagian*
    Section chief

24. **Daigaku**　　　　　　　*Universiti*
    University

25. **Gakkō**　　　　　　　　*Sekolah*
    School

26. **Yōchien**　　　　　　　*Tadika*
    Kindergarten ·

27. **Shōgakkō**　　　　　　*Sekolah rendah*
    Primary school

28. **Chūgakkō**　　　　　　*Sekolah Menengah Rendah*
    Junior High School

29. **Kōtōgakkō**　　　　　　*Sekolah Tinggi*
    High School

30. **Gōkaku**　　　　　　　*Lulus*
    Pass

31. **Ukemasu**　　　　　　　*Lulus (perbuatan)*
    Pass (verb)

32. **Fugōkaku**　　　　　　*Gagal*
    Fail

33. **Shūshi**　　　　　　　　*Sarjana*
    Masters

34. **Hakushi**　　　　　　　*Doktor Falsafah*
    Doctor of Philosophy
    (Ph. D)

A. *Isikan tempat-tempat kosong.*
Fill in the blanks.

Gantinama Pronouns	*Saya* I ————	*Kamu* You ————	*Dia (perempuan)* She ————	*Dia (laki-laki)* He ————	*Kita* We ————
Angka Numerals	2 ———— 0 ————	4 ———— 13 ————	6 ———— 30 ————	8 ———— 101 ————	9 ———— 718 ————
Hari dalam minggu Days of the week	*Ahad* Sunday ————	*Selasa* Tuesday ————	*Rabu* Wednesday ————	*Sabtu* Saturday ————	*Jumaat* Friday ————
Warna Colour	*Merah* Red ———— Nezumiro	**Aoi** *Hijau* Green ————	*Hitam* Black ———— Murasaki	*Kuning* Yellow ———— Momoiro	*Putih* White ———— Chairo

Haribulan Days of the month	*1hb* 1st	*3hb* 3rd	*7hb* 7th	*8hb* 8th	*9hb* 9th
	20hb 20th	*23hb* 23rd	*25hb* 25th	*30hb* 30th	*31hb* 31st
Bulan Months	*Januari* January	*April* April	*Jun* June	*Disember* December	*November* November
	Ogos August	*September* September	*Februari* February	*Mac* March	*Julai* July
Proposisi (tempat) Location	*Dalam* Inside	*Atas* Top	*Sebelah* Beside	*Bawah* Under	*Belakang* Behind
	Depan Front	*Di sini* Here	*Di sana* There	*Sebelah sana* Over there	*Di* In
	Di At	*Mana* Where	*Sebelah sana* Over there	*Jauh* Far	*Dekat* Near

Anggota badan manusia Parts of the Human body	*Kepala* Head	*Perut* Stomach	*Gigi* Teeth	*Tangan* Hand	*Kaki* Leg
	————	————	————	————	————
	Mulut Mouth	*Mata* Eyes	*Pergelangan* Ankle	*Kerongkong* Throat	*Jari* Finger
	————	————	————	————	————

	Paruparu Lung	*Gelembong* Bladder	*Jantung* Heart	*Usus* Intestines	*Appendictis* Appendicitis	*Dada* Chest
Pekerjaan Professions	*Doktor* Doctor	*Peguam* Lawyer	*Jururawat* Nurse	*Guru* Teacher	*Jurutera* Engineer	*Pelajar* Student
	Pengurus Manager	*Ketua bahagian* Section chief	*Pekerja syarikat* Company workers	*Pelakon (laki-laki)* Actor	*Pelakon (wanita)* Actress	*Penyanyi* Singer
Keturunan Nationality	*Jepun* Japanese	*Malaysia* Malaysian	*Singapura* Singaporean	*Amerika* American	*Jerman* German	*Belanda* Dutch
	Makan Eat	*Minum* Drink	*Bangun* Get up	*Tidur* Sleep	*Kerja* Work	*Rehat* Rest
Katakerja Verbs	*Kahwin* Marry	*Pandu* Drive	*Bersih* Clean	*Hantar* Send	*Kelahi* Quarrel	*Jumpa* Meet
	Cakap Talk	*Buka* Open	*Tutup* Close	*Memasang suis* Switch on	*Memadam suis* Switch off	*Duduk* Sit

	Lihat See	*Dengar* Listen	*Tulis* Write	*Berbau* To smell	*Pertunangan* To get engaged	*Ambil* Take
Adjektif Adjectives	*Cantik* Beautiful	*Sedikit* Small	*Besar* Big	*Murah* Cheap	*Mahal* Expensive	*Keras* Hard
	Lembut Soft	*Susah* Difficult	*Lebar* Wide	*Sempit* Narrow	*Gelap* Dark	*Terang* Bright
Adverba Adverbs	*Berbagai* Various	*Perlahan-lahan* Slowly	*Baik* Well	*Kecil* Little	*Terbaik* Best	*Sudah* Already
	Serta-merta At once	*Selalu* Always	*Hampir* Almost	*Mungkin* May be	*Kadang-kadang* Sometimes	*Belum lagi* Not yet
Peralatan Stationery	*Pen* Pen	*Kertas* Paper	*Pensil* Pencil	*Buku Surat* Letter pad	*Sampul Surat* Envelope	*Surat* Letter

Pakaian Things to wear	*Baju* Shirt	*Kasut* Shoes	*Seluar* Trousers	*Topi* Cap, hat	*Pakaian sepasang* Clothes	*Sarung kaki* Socks
Cuaca, Musim Weather, Seasons	*Panas* Hot	*Sejuk* Cold	*Sejuk (dingin)* Cool	*Panas* Warm	*Angin* Wind	*Hujan* Rain
	Salji Snow	*Musim bunga* Spring	*Musim panas* Summer	*Musim gugur* Autumn	*Musim dingin* Winter	*Musim hujan* Rainy season
	Berangin Windy	*Taufan* Typhoon	*Banjir* Flood	*Hujan renyai-renyai* Light rain (drizzle)	*Hujan lebat* Heavy rain	*Hari baik* Fine day
Rasa Taste	*Mamis* Sweet	*Masin* Salty	*Masam* Sour	*Pahit* Bitter	*Lazat (berempah)* Spicy	*Lazat* Delicious

B. Dōshi — Katakerja
Verbs

Isikan tempat-tempat kosong.
Fill in the blanks.

Kata sekarang Present tense	Kata lampau Past tense	Kata lampau (negatif) Past tense negative	Bentuk suruhan (halus) Please (form)	Bentuk suruhan negatif (halus) Please (negative)
Tabemasu				
	Urimashita			
			Katte kudasai	
Okimasu				
				Nenaide kudasai
		Kakimasen deshita		
	Hatarakimashita		Nonde kudasai	
		Machimasen deshita		
Kekkon shimasu				

	Moraimashita	Yomimasen deshita	Unten shite kudasai	Ryori shinaide kudasai
Yomimasu	*Mesti* Must	*Jika* If	*Walaupun* Even if	*Keinginan* Desire
Ikimasu				
Kimasu				
Akemasu	Shimenakereba narimasen	Tottara	Hanashite mo	
Yasumimasu	Minakereba narimasen			Sagashitai

	Yametara		Suzukete mo		Unten shitai
		Shinpai shitara		Sōji shite mo	
Sanpo shimasu					

C. *Beritahu apa anda lakukan hari ini.*
   Tell what you did today.

D. *Isikan tempat-tempat kosong.*
   Fill in the blanks.

(a) **tegami o** _____ (wrote) *telah menulis*

(b) **denwa o** _____ (to telephone) *menelefon*

(c) **nodo ga** _____ (to have a sore throat) *mendapat sakit kerongkong*

(d) **onaka ga** _____ (hungry) *lapar*

(e) **kaze ga** _____ (caught) *telah menghidap*

(f) **ame ga** _____ (is raining) *sedang hujan*

(g) **airon o** _____ (to iron) *menggosok (kain)*

(h) **isha o** _____ (called) *telah dipanggil*

(i) **dēnpo o** _____ (please send) *tolong hantar*

(j) **kiite o** _____ (bought) *telah membeli*

E. *Apa kata anda?*
   What do you say?

(a) *Apabila anda mengucapkan tahniah kepada seseorang.*
    When you congratulate someone.

(b) *Apabila anda minta maaf.*
    When you apologise.

(c) *Apabila anda mengenalkan diri.*
    When you introduce yourself.

(d) *Apabila anda memasuki rumah orang.*
When you enter someone's house.

(e) *Apabila anda meminta seseorang bercakap dengan perlahan-lahan.*
When you ask someone to speak slowly.

(f) *Apabila anda mula makan.*
When you are about to start eating.

(g) *Mengucapkan terima kasih kepada tuan rumah atas makanan.*
When you thank your host for the food.

(h) *Apabila anda meminta seseorang supaya cepat.*
When you ask someone to hurry up.

(i) *Apabila anda lewat.*
When you are late.

(j) *Apabila anda mengucapkan selamat tinggal.*
When you say goodbye.

(k) *Apabila anda meminta seseorang supaya berjalan terus.*
When you ask someone to go straight ahead.

(l) *Apabila anda meminta seseorang supaya berpusing ke kanan.*
When you ask someone to turn right.

(m) *Apabila anda bertanya seseorang di mana ia tinggal.*
When you ask someone where he lives.

(n) *Apabila anda ingin tahu tempat anda berada.*
When you want to know the place where you are.

(o) *Hendak mengetahui harga sesuatu barang.*
When you want to know the price of something.

(p) *Anda meminta seseorang panggilkan teksi.*
When you ask someone to call the taxi.

F. *Tukarkan dalam bahasa Jepun.*
   Change into Japanese.

(a) *Adakah jalan ini menghala ke Singapura?*
    Does this road lead to Singapore?

(b) *Bilik ini sempit.*
    This room is narrow.

(c) *Tokyo lebih besar dari Osaka.*
    Tokyo is bigger than Osaka.

(d) *Perak tidak begitu mahal seperti emas.*
    Silver is not as expensive as gold.

(e) *Sila datang pada pukul 2.10 petang.*
    Please come at 2.10 p.m.

(f) *Pukul berapa anda akan balik?*
    What time will you return?

(g) *Tolong bawakan buku itu ke sini.*
    Please bring the books here.

(h) *Saya pergi ke pejabat pos untuk menghantar suatu bungkusan.*
    I went to the post-office (for the purpose) of sending a parcel.

(i) *Apakah perkataan bahasa Jepun bagi 'biru'?*
    What is the Japanese word for 'blue'?

(j) *Jika anda tidak mempunyai wang, anda tidak boleh membeli apa-apa.*
    If you don't have money, you cannot buy anything.

(k) *Ia mengambil masa lebih kurang 10 minit dengan kereta.*
    It takes about 10 minutes by car.

(l) *Walaupun anda bercakap dengan perlahan, saya tidak boleh memahaminya.*
    Even if you speak slowly, I cannot understand.

(m) *Anda boleh membuat tempahan menerusi telefon.*
    You can make the reservations by phone.

Daijūshichika - Dōshi
Pelajaran 17 – Katakerja
Lesson 17 – Verbs

Pelajaran ini memberikan bentuk kamus dan bentuk biasa beberapa katakerja yang telah digunakan dalam buku ini. Bentuk biasa itu berguna kerana ia digunakan secara luas dalam bahasa harian Jepun.

This lesson gives the dictionary form and the plain form of some of the verbs used in this book. The plain form is useful as it is commonly used in the daily language of the Japanese.

Kata sekarang Present Tense	*Bentuk kamus* Dictionary Form	*Kata lampau* Past Tense	*Kata lampau (negatif)* Past Negative	*Kata sekarang (negatif)* Present Negative	*Kata sekarang (berterusan)* Present Continuous	*Kata lampau (berterusan)* Past Continuous	*Harus (mesti)* Must
		… mashita … ta … da	… masen deshita … nakatta	… masen … nai	… teimasu … teiru	… teimashita … teitta	… nakereba narimasen … nakuccha
ikimasu	iku	ikimashita itta	ikimasen deshita ikanakatta	ikimasen ikanai	itteimasu itteiru	itteimashita itteitta	ikanakereba narimasen ikanakuccha
yomimasu	yomu	yomimashita yonda	yomimasen deshita yomanakatta	yomimasen yomanai	yondeimasu yondeiru	yondeimashita yondeitta	yomanakereba narimasen yomanakuccha
nomimasu	nomu	nomimashita nonda	nomimasen deshita nomanakatta	nomimasen nomanai	nondeimasu nondeiru	nondeimashita nondeitta	nomanakereba narimasen nomanakuccha

mimasu	miru	mimashita / mita	mimasen deshita / minakatta	mimasen / minai	miteimasu / miteiru	miteimashita / miteitta	minakereba / narimasen / minakuccha
arukimasu	aruku	arukimashita / aruita	arukimasen deshita / arukanakatta	arukimasen / arukanai	aruiteimasu / aruiteiru	aruiteimashita / aruiteitta	arukanakereba / narimasen / arukanakuccha
hairimasu	hairu	hairimashita / haita	hairimasen deshita / hairanakatta	hairimasen / hairanai	haiteimasu / haiteiru	haiteimashita / haiteitta	hairanakereba / narimasen / hairanakuccha
tachimasu	tatsu	tachimashita / tatta	tachimasen deshita / tattanakatta	tachimasen / tattanai	tatteimasu / tatteiru	tatteimashita / tatteitta	tattanakereba / narimasen / tattanakuccha
dashimasu	dasu	dashimashita / dashita	dashimasen deshita / dasanakatta	dashimasen / dasanai	dashiteimasu / dashiteiru	dashiteimashita / dashiteitta	dasanakereba / narimasen / dasanakuccha
benkyō shimasu	benkyō suru	benkyō shimashita / benkyō shita	benkyō shimasen deshita / benkyō shinakatta	benkyō shimasen / benkyō shinai	benkyō shiteimasu / benkyō shiteiru	benkyō shiteimashita / benkyō shiteitta	benkyō shinakereba / narimasen / benkyō shinakuccha

Kata sekarang Present Tense	Bentuk kamus Dictionary Form	Kata lampau Past Tense	Kata lampau (negatif) Past Negative	Kata sekarang (negatif) Present Negative	Kata sekarang (berterusan) Present Continuous	Kata lampau (berterusan) Past Continuous	Harus (mesti) Must
kekkon shimasu	kekkon suru	kekkon shimashita kekkon shita	kekkon shimasen deshita kekkon shinakatta	kekkon shimasen kekkon shinai	kekkon shiteimasu kekkon shiteiru	kekkon shiteimashita kekkon shiteitta	kekkon shinakereba narimasen kekkon shinakuccha
unten shimasu	unten suru	unten shimashita unten shita	unten shimasen deshita unten shinakatta	unten shimasen unten shinai	unten shiteimasu unten shiteiru	unten shiteimashita unten shiteitta	unten shinakereba narimasen unten shinakuccha
nemasu	neru	nemashita neta	nemasen deshita nenakatta	nemasen nenai	neteimasu neteiru	neteimashita neteitta	nenakereba narimasen nenakuccha
hakobimasu	hakobu	hakobimashita hakonda	hakobimasen deshita hakobanakatta	hakobimasen hakobanai	hakondeimasu hakondeiru	hakondeimashita hakondeitta	hokobanakereba narimasen hakobanakuccha
machimasu	matsu	machimashita matta	machimasen deshita mattanakatta	machimasen mattanai	matteimasu matteiru	matteimashita matteitta	mattanakereba narimasen mattanakuccha
wakarimasu	wakaru	wakarimashita wakata	wakarimasen deshita wakaranakatta	wakarimasen wakaranai	wakateimasu wakateiru	wakateimashita wakateitta	wakaranakereba narimasen wakaranakuccha
oshiemasu	oshieru	oshiemashita oshieta	oshiemasen deshita oshienakatta	oshiemasen oshienai	oshieteimasu oshietteiru	oshieteimashita oshieteitta	oshienakereba narimasen oshienakuccha
wasuremasu	wasureru	wasuremashita wasureta	wasuremasen deshita wasurenakatta	wasuremasen wasurenai	wasureteimasu wasureteiru	wasureteimashita wasureteitta	wasurenakereba narimasen wasurenakuccha

A. *Berikan bentuk biasa dalam bahasa Jepun bagi perkataan-perkataan berikut.*

Give the plain forms of the following words in Japanese.

1. *(sedang) makan*
   eating
2. *(sedang) minum*
   drinking
3. *(sudah) makan*
   ate
4. *(sedang) bangun*
   waking up
5. *(sedang) melihat*
   seeing
6. *(telah) mendengar*
   heard
7. *tidak duduk*
   did not sit
8. *tidak berdiri*
   did not stand
9. *tidak akan memandu*
   will not drive
10. *tidak akan berkahwin*
    will not marry

11. *telah membeli*
    bought
12. *telah dijual*
    sold
13. *mengira*
    count
14. *tidak kira*
    did not count
15. *mesti menghantar*
    must send
16. *mesti pergi*
    must go
17. *mesti membaca*
    must read
18. *ingat*
    remember
19. *fikir*
    think
20. *berjalan*
    walk

B. *Berikan bentuk biasa bagi perkataan-perkataan berikut.*
Give the plain form of the following words.

Bentuk kamus Dictionary Form	*Kata lampau* Past Tense	*Kata lampau (negatif)* Past Negative	*Kata sekarang (negatif)* Present Negative	*Kata sekarang (berterusan)* Present Continuous	*Kata lampau (berterusan)* Past Continuous	*Harus (mesti)* Must
aruku						
	shimeta					
		tabenakatta				
			hakobanai			
				suwateiru		
					sōjishiteitta	
						konakuccha
					hanashiteitta	
	shiranakatta					
sanpo suru						

Daijūhakka – Fukushi, Keiyōshi
Pelajaran 18 – Adverba, Adjektif
Lesson 18 – Adverbs, Adjectives

Pelajaran ini memberi adverba dan adjektif yang selalu digunakan dalam Bahasa Jepun. Adalah berfaedah untuk mengingatkannya.

This lesson gives a list of commonly used adverbs and adjectives in the Japanese language. It will be useful to memorize them.

Fukushi Adverbs	*Adverba*
1. **Chotto** A moment	*Seketika*
2. **Shukoshi** A little, A few	*Sedikit*
3. **Takusan** A lot, Much	*Banyak*
4. **Taihen, Totemo** Very	*Sangat*
5. **Mezurashii (ku)** Rare (ly)	*Jarang*
6. **Itsumo** Always	*Selalu*
7. **Tabitabi** Often	*Sering kali, Kerap kali*
8. **Tokidoki** Sometimes	*Kadang-kadang*
9. **Mō** Already	*Sudah, Telah*

10. **Mada**
Yet, Still
Belum, Masih

11. **Yukkuri**
• Slowly
Secara perlahan

12. **Hayaku**
Quickly
Secara cepat

13. **Iroiro**
Various
Berbagai

14. **Ichiban**
Best
Terbaik

15. **Saisho**
First
Pertama

16. **Saigo**
Last
Terakhir

17. **Zuibun**
Considerable
Boleh dipertimbangkan

18. **Zehi**
By all means
Dengan senang hati

19. **Yoku**
Well
Sihat

20. **Tabun**
Perhaps
Mungkin

21. **Kitto**
Surely
Tentu, Pasti

22. **Amari**
Not very, Not so
Tidak banyak, Tidak begitu

23. **Yori**
More than
Lebih dari

24. **Zenzen** Entirely	*Keseluruhannya*
25. **Sugu** Soon	*Secepat mungkin*
26. **Motto** More	*Lebih*
27. **Zettai** Definitely	*Pasti*
Keiyōshi Adjectives	*Adjektif*
1. **Ōkii** Big	*Besar*
2. **Chiisai** Small	*Kecil*
3. **Takai** Expensive, Tall	*Mahal, Tinggi*
4. **Yasui** Cheap	*Murah*
5. **Yoi (ii)** Good	*Baik*
6. **Warui** Bad	*Buruk*
7. **Furui** Old	*Lama*
8. **Atarashii** New	*Baru*
9. **Hiroi** Wide	*Lebar*

10. **Semai** Narrow	*Sempit*
11. **Omoi** Heavy	*Berat*
12. **Karui** Light	*Ringan*
13. **Oishii** Delicious	*Sedap*
14. **Mazui** Tasteless	*Tiada rasa*
15. **Amai** Sweet	*Manis*
16. **Karai** Salty	*Masin*
17. **Muzukashii** Difficult	*Susah*
18. **Yasashii, Kantan** Easy	*Mudah*
19. **Atsui** Hot	*Panas*
20. **Samui** Cold	*Sejuk*
21. **Osoi** Late	*Lambat*
22. **Hayai** Early	*Awal*
23. **Utsukushii, Kirei** Beautiful	*Cantik*

24. **Minikui**　　　　　　　　*Hodoh*
    Ugly

25. **Tōi**　　　　　　　　　*Jauh*
    Far

26. **Chikaku**　　　　　　　*Dekat*
    Near

27. **Nagai**　　　　　　　　*Panjang*
    Long

28. **Mijikai**　　　　　　　*Pendek*
    Short

29. **Kirei**　　　　　　　　*Bersih*
    Clean

30. **Kitanai**　　　　　　　*Kotor*
    Dirty

31. **Shiawase**　　　　　　*Kegembiraan*
    Happiness

32. **Kanashii**　　　　　　*Sedih*
    Sad

33. **Shizuka**　　　　　　　*Senyap*
    Quiet

34. **Sawagashii, Yakamashii**　　*Bising*
    Noisy

35. **Suzushii**　　　　　　*Dingin*
    Cool

36. **Atatakai**　　　　　　*Panas*
    Warm

37. **Omoshiroi**　　　　　*Menarik*
    Interesting

38. **Tsumaranai** Dull	*Bosan*
39. **Kurushii** Suffer	*Menderita*
40. **Sabishii** Lonely	*Kesepian*
41. **Hazukashii** Shy, Shame	*Malu*
42. **Tanoshii** Pleasant	*Menyenangkan*
43. **Ureshi** Glad, Joyful	*Gembira*
44. **Itai** Painful	*Sakit*
45. **Kawaii** Cute	*Comel*
46. **Subarashii** Wonderful	*Indah*

A. *Berikan perkataan berlawanan untuk perkataan-perkataan yang berikut dalam Bahasa Jepun.*
Give the opposite of the following words in Japanese.

a. *Seringkali, Selalu*
Often

b. *Sudah, Telah*
Already

c. *Pertama*
First

d. *Perlahan-lahan*
Slowly

e. *Mungkin*
Perhaps

f. *Besar*
Big

g. *Murah*
Cheap

h. *Lebar*
Wide

i. *Manis*
Sweet

j. *Sejuk*
Cold

k. *Dingin*
Cool

l. *Lambat*
Late

m. *Cantik*
Beautiful

n. *Pendek*
Short

o. *Jauh*
Far

p. *Sedap*
Delicious

q. *Senyap*
Quiet

r. *Menarik*
Interesting

s. *Berat*
Heavy

t. *Lama*
Old

B. *Buat ayat dengan perkataan-perkataan berikut:*
Make sentences with the following words:

(a) **Chotto**

(b) **Takusan**

(c) **Mezurashii**

(d) **Mada**

(e) **Yori**

(f) **Yoku**

(g) **Zettai**

(h) **Saigo**

(i) **Saisho**

(j) **Iroiro**

(k) **Sabishii**

(l) **Tanoshii**

(m) **Kitanai**

Jawapan kepada Latihan
Answers to Exercises

Dainika – Nichijō Kaiwa
Pelajaran 2 – Percakapan Sehari-hari
Lesson 2 – Daily Conversation

A.

A: **Ogenki desu ka?**
B: **Hai, genki desu, dōmo arigatō.**
   Okage sama de genki desu.
   Anata wa do desu ka?
A: **Hai, genki desu, dōmo arigatō.**
B: **Taro sensei wa genki desu ka?**
A: **Hai, Taro sensei wa genki desu.**
B: **Anata wa isogashii desu ka?**
A: **Hai, watashi wa isogashii desu.**
   Iie, watashi wa isogashii ja arimasen.
B: **Kore wa pen desu ka?**
A: **Hai, kore wa pen desu.**
   Iie, kore wa pen ja arimasen.
B: **Anata no hon desu ka?**
   Hai, watashi no hon desu.
   Iie, watashi no hon ja arimasen.

B.

1. *Selamat pagi.*   **Ohāyo gozaimasu.**
   Good morning.
2. *Selamat tengahari.*   **Konnichi wa.**
   Good afternoon.
3. *Selamat petang.*   **Konban wa.**
   Good evening.
4. *Apa khabar?*   **Ogenki desu ka?**
   How are you?

5. *Tahniah.*   **Omedetō.**
   Congratulations.
6. *Selamat Tahun Baru.*   **Shinen omedetō gozaimasu.**
   Happy New Year.
7. *Selamat malam.*   **Oyasumi nasai.**
   Good night.
8. *Sama-sama*   **Dōitashi mashite.**
   Please don't mention.

.C.
1. wa, ka
2. wa, desu
3. wa, ja (dewa) arimasen
4. desu, ka, desu, ka
5. omedetō

Daisanka – Nichijō Kaiwa
Pelajaran 3 – Perbualan Harian
Lesson 3 – Daily Conversation

A.
A: Anata wa Marēishia jin desu ka?
B: Hai, watashi wa Marēishia jin desu.
A: Doko ni sundeimasu ka?
B: (Ōsaka) ni sundeimasu.
A: Doko de hatarakimasu ka?
B: Matsushita de hatarakimasu.
A: Kyō wa atsui desu ne?
B: Hai, kyō wa atsui desu.
   Iie, kyō wa atsui ja arimasen.
A: Kinō wa samui deshita ka?
B: Hai, kinō wa samui deshita.
   Iie, kinō wa samui ja arimasen deshita.
A: Kekkon shimashita ka?
B: Hai, kekkon shimashita.
   Iie, dokushin desu.
   Iie, mada kekkon shimasen.

B.

1. Kore wa bōrupen deshita.
2. Ano hito wa sensei deshita.
3. Kyō wa isogashii ja arimasen deshita.
4. Kanojo wa hima deshita.
5. Kyō wa atsui ja arimasen deshita.
6. Marēishia jin wa kirei deshita.
7. Kare wa Taro san ja arimasen deshita.
8. Donata wa Taro san deshita ka?
9. Anata no kaisha wa doko deshita ka?
10. Kore wa donata no enpitsu deshita ka?
11. Anata wa doko de hatarakimashita ka?
12. Wakarimashita ka?
13. Itsu kekkon shimashita ka?
14. Doko ni sumimashita ka?

C.

1. Anata wa doko de hatarakimasu ka?
2. Kono kata wa Taro san desu.
3. Watashi no tomodachi wa sensei ja arimasen.
4. Kare wa Nihon jin desu ka?
5. Naze Tōkyō ni ikimashita ka?
6. Itsu kekkon shimashita ka?
7. Watashi wa jidōsha de ikimashita.
8. Hai, genki desu, dōmo arigatō.

Daiyonka – Kyoshitsu de
Pelajaran 4 – Di Bilik Darjah
Lesson 4 – In the Classroom

A.

A: Anata wa Nihon jin desu ka?
B: Iie, Watashi wa Nihonjin ja (dewa) arimasen.
   Marēishia jin desu.
A: Nihon go o hanashimasu ka?
B: Hai, chotto hanashimasu.

A: Anata no namae o kaite kudasai.
B: Kore wa watashi no namae desu.
Dōzo yonde kudasai.
A: Anata no Nihon go no sensei wa donata san desu ka?
B: Kato sensei desu.
A: Mō ichido osshatte kudasai.
B: Kato sensei desu.
Kare o shiteimasu ka?
A: Iie, shirimasen.
B: Kare wa asoko ni imasu.
Dōzo kare to atte kudasai.

B san wa Kato sensei ni: Kono kata wa A san desu.
A: Hajimemashite. Watashi wa A desu. Dōzo yoroshiku.
Kato Sensei: Kochira koso, dōzo yoroshiku.
Dōzo, suwate kudasai.
B: Dōmo arigatō.

B.
1. Omatase shimashita.
2. Mō ichido osshate kudasai.
3. Ohairi kudasai.
Haite kudasai.
Dōzo haite kudasai.
4. Okake kudasai.
Suwate kudasai.
5. Hajimemashite. Watashi wa _____ desu. Dōzo yoroshiku.
6. Chotto wakarimasu (wakarimashita).
7. Kotaete kudasai.
8. Motto ōkina koe de itte kudasai.
9. Nihon go wa wakarimasu ka?
10. (i) Shinen omedetō gozaimasu.
(ii) Konban wa.
(iii) Oyasumi nasai.

C.

Kata sekarang Present Tense	Bentuk kamus Dictionary Form	Kata sekarang (negatif) Present Negative	Bentuk suruhan (halus) Please Form
kotaemasu	kotaeru	kotaemasen	kotaete kudasai
hairimasu	hairu	hairimasen	haite kudasai
ikimasu	iku	ikimasen	itte kudasai
hatarakimasu	hataraku	hatarakimasen	hataraite kudasai
yomimasu	yomu	yomimasen	yonde kudasai
hanashimasu	hanasu	hanashimasen	hanashite kudasai
mimasu	miru	mimasen	mite kudasai
kekkon shimasu	kekkon suru	kekkon shimasen	kekkon shite kudasai
kakimasu	kaku	kakimasen	kaite kudasai
shitsumon shimasu	shitsumon suru	shitsumon shimasen	shitsumon shite kudasai

Daigoka – Kazu, Toki
Pelajaran 5 – Nombor, Masa
Lesson 5 – Number, Time

A.

A: Ima nanji desu ka?
B: 3 (san)ji desu.
A: Anata no tokei wa atteimasu ka?
B: Hai, so desu.
A: Iie, anata no tokei wa susundeimasu.
B: So desu ka?
A: Hai, so desu.
B: Nanpun susundeimasu ka?
A: Jūpun desu.

B.
1. Ichinichi wa nijūyojikan desu ka?
2. (Watashi wa) okimasen deshita.
3. Ichijikan wa nanpun arimasu ka?
4. C kara D made, basu de nanjikan kakarimasu ka?
5. 5 (Gojikan) kakarimasu.
6. Kare wa gogo 3 (san)ji made tabemasen deshita.
7. Ichibanme no hito wa koko ni suwate kudasai.
8. Kono kaisha wa anata no kaisha no yonbun no ichi desu.

C.

Bentuk kamus Dictionary Form	Kata lampau (negatif) Past Negative
hairu	hairimasen deshita
suwaru	suwarimasen deshita
shiru	shirimasen deshita
oshieru	oshiemasen deshita
benkyō suru	benkyō shimasen deshita
wakaru	wakarimasen deshita
aru	arimasen deshita
kuru	kimasen deshita
neru	nemasen deshita
kazoeru	kazoemasen deshita
tsukareru	tsukaremasen deshita
kaeru	kaerimasen deshita

Dairokka – Sūshi
Pelajaran 6 – Angka
Lesson 6 – The Numerals

A.
1. nimai
2. santo, happiki (hachihiki), santo
3. roppon, gomai

4. jūssatsu, sanbai
5. nihiki, sanbiki
6. jūnin, futari, hachinin
7. nisoku, happon (hachihon)
8. ichidai
9. ko
10. nihai

B.

1. Nan*satsu*	6. Nan*ko*
2. Nan*zoku*	7. Nan*chaku*
3. Nan*bai*	8. Nan*dai*
4. Nan*biki*	9. Nan*seki*
5. Nan*to*	10. Nan*ki*

C.

Bentuk kamus Dictionary Form	*Kemahuan* Desire
kau	kaitai
shiru	shiritai
deru	detai
uru	uritai
kaeru	kaeritai
iku	ikitai
akeru	aketai
konyaku suru	konyaku shitai
isogu	isogitai
okiru	okitai

Daishichika – Hi, Shū, Gatsu
Pelajaran 7 – Hari, minggu, dan bulan
dalam sesuatu tahun
Lesson 7 – Days, Week, and Month
of the Year

A.

A: Kyō wa nanyōbi desu ka?
B: Kyō wa kayōbi desu.
A: Tan san no tanjōbi wa itsu desu ka?
B: Raishū no getsuyōbi desu.
A: Kongetsu wa nangatsu desu ka?
B: Hachigatsu desu.
A: Raigetsu wa nangatsu desu ka?
B: Kugatsu desu.
A: Sengetsu wa nangatsu deshita ka?
B: Shichi gatsu deshita.
A: Ishūkan ni wa nannichikan arimasu ka?
B: Nanokakan desu.

B.
1. no, desu.
2. wa, deshita.
3. no, no, wa, to.
4. no, wa, ni(e), ka.
5. wa, ka.
6. kara, made.
7. wa, no, no.
8. kara, made, to, ga.
9. ni.
10. no, wa, no, wa.

C:

Bentuk kamus Dictionary Form	Bentuk jemputan (bolehkah kita) Invitational
sanpo suru	sanpo shimashyoo (ka)
iku	ikimashyoo (ka)
hajimeru	hajimemashyoo (ka)
isogu	isogimashyoo (ka)
kazoeru	kazoemashyoo (ka)
konyaku suru	konyaku shimashyoo (ka)
miru	mimashyoo (ka)
matsu	machimashyoo (ka)
kaku	kakimashyoo (ka)
yobu	yobimashyoo (ka)

Daihakka – Fukushū
Pelajaran 8 – Latihan Ulangkaji
Lesson 8 – Review Exercises

A.

1.	j	6.	e
2.	i	7.	d
3.	h	8.	a
4.	g	9.	b
5.	f	10.	c

B.

1.	e	6.	c
2.	g	7.	b
3.	d	8.	f
4.	j	9.	a
5.	i	10.	h

C.
1. Watashi wa Nihon go o narateimasu.
2. Kore wa nan desu ka?
3. Kinō wa atsui deshita ka?
4. Anata wa doko ni sundeimasu ka?
5. Kono kata wa watashi no sensei desu.
6. Watashi wa ichigatsu kara sangatsu made ni, Nihon ni ikimashita.
7. Ashita wa nanyōbi desu ka?
8. Ichi nen ni nannichi arimasu ka?
9. Nihon go wa muzukashii ja arimasen.
10. Senshū kare wa Nihon ni ikimashita.

D.
1. Kore wa nan desu ka?
2. Anata wa Nihon go o hanashimasu ka?
3. Anata wa doko de hatarakimasu ka?
4. Anata wa itsu kekkon shimashita ka?
5. Naze anata wa Nihon go o benkyō shimasu ka?
6. Watashi wa senshū Nihon ni ikimashita.
7. Ima nanji desu ka?
8. Kyō wa nanyōbi desu ka?
9. Watashi no tanjōbi wa ichigatsu yokka desu.
10. Ashita ni aimashyoo ka?

E.
1. Omatase shimashita.
2. Dōzo okake kudasai.
   Dōzo suwate kudasai.
3. Mō ichido osshate kudasai.
4. Chotto ma te kudasai.
   Shōsho omachi kudasai.
5. Motto ōkina koe de itte kudasai.

F.
1. Jū
2. Jūsan
3. Jūshichi (Jūnana)
4. Nijūichi
5. Sanjūichi
6. Nihyaku nanajūyon
7. Sambyaku nijūroku
8. Sen
9. Asa goji gofun sugi
10. Gogo niji han
11. Asa hachiji jūgofun sugi
12. Hachiji jūpun mae
13. Rokuji jūnifun mae
14. Getsuyōbi
15. Suiyōbi
16. Kinyōbi
17. Doyōbi
18. Shigatsu
19. Gogatsu
20. Jūgatsu
21. Jūnigatsu
22. Tsuitachi
23. Mikka
24. Tōka
25. Hatsuka
26. Nijūshichi nichi
27. Ikkagetsu
28. Gokagetsu
29. Shichikagetsu
    (Nanakagetsu)
30. Jūkagetsu

G.

Kata sekarang Present Tense	Bentuk kamus Dictionary Form	Kata lampau Past Tense	Kata lampau (negatif) Past Negative	Keinginan Desire
wakarimasu	wakaru	wakarimashita	wakarimasen deshita	wakaritai
ikimasu	iku	ikimashita	ikimasen deshita	ikitai
benkyō shimasu	benkyō suru	benkyō shimashita	benkyō shimasen deshita	benkyō shitai
mimasu	miru	mimashita	mimasen deshita	mitai
kikimasu	kiku	kikimashita	kikimasen deshita	kikitai
nemasu	neru	nemashita	nemasen deshita	netai
kaerimasu	kaeru	kaerimashita	kaerimasen deshita	kaeritai
demasu	deru	demashita	demasen deshita	detai
owarimasu	owaru	owarimashita	owarimasen deshita	owaritai
sanpo shimasu	sanpo suru	sanpo shimashita	sanpo shimasen deshita	sanpo shitai
arukimasu	aruku	arukimashita	arukimasen deshita	arukitai
hashirimasu	hashiru	hashirimashita	hashirimasen deshita	hashiritai
hajimemasu	hajimeru	hajimemashita	hajimemasen deshita	hajimetai
haraimasu	harau	haraimashita	haraimasen deshita	haraitai
kaimasu	kau	kaimashita	kaimasen deshita	kaitai

Daikyuka – Nichijō Seikatsu
Pelajaran 9 – Kehidupan harian
Lesson 9 – Daily Life

B.
1. Watashi wa maiasa shichiji ni okimasu.
2. Okite kara, ha ga migakimasu.
3. Tokidoki osoku made hatarakimasu.
4. Hon o yondari, eiga o mitari, kaimono o shitari shimasu.
5. Tokidoki kaisha ni basu de ikimasu.
6. Uchi ni kaete kara, ofuro o hairimasu.
7. Watashi wa mainichi hatarakimasu.
8. Watashi wa yoku hatarakimasu kara, tsukaremasu.
9. Kyūryō wa ikura desu ka?
10. Kyō wa ha ga migakimasen deshita.

C.
1. Mainichi wa rokuji ni okimasu.
2. Hiruyasumi wa nanji kara desu ka?
3. Ima wa nani o shimasu ka?
4. Doyōbi to nichiyōbi ga yasumi desu.
5. Maiban wa nanji goro ni nemasu ka?

Daijukka – Kaimono
Pelajaran 10 – Membeli-belah
Lesson 10 – Shopping

C.

Bentuk kamus Dictionary Form	Bentuk suruhan (halus) Please Form
yomu	yonde kudasai
tatsu	tatte kudasai
todokeru	todokete kudasai
nomu	nonde kudasai
yobu	yonde kudasai
oyogu	oyonde kudasai
miru	mite kudasai
makeru	makete kudasai
kiku	kiite kudasai
kaku	kaite kudasai

Daijūika – (i) Hoteru   (ii) Geshukuya
Pelajaran 11 – (i) Hotel   (ii) Rumah Tumpangan
Lesson 11 – (i) Hotel   (ii) Boarding House

A.
1. no, ni, ga, ka
2. no, ni, to, ga
3. o (ga)
4. ni (wa), ga
5. wa(ga), desu
6. wa, desu, ka
7. wa, desu
8. ga, desu, ka, to, desu, ka
9. kara
10. ni (e)

11. no, ni
12. ji, ji
13. wa
14. wa, de, to, ka
15. yori
16. no, wa, ni, ka
17. o (ga), ka
18. desu
19. wa (ni), ka
20. yori

B.
1. Doko no hoteru ga suki desu ka? Kore to (sore) are desu ka?
2. Shizukana heya ga arimasu ka?
3. Hikoki wa kyō no gogo goji ni shuppatsu shimasu.
4. Ashita no asa wa watashi ni denwa o shite kudasai.
5. Obenjō wa nikai ni arimasu.
6. Obenjō wa engawa no soba ni arimasu.
7. Kyō wa futsuka to mikka desu ka?
8. Hotel wa (ga) Nihon go de nan to iimasu ka?
9. Watashi wa asa hachiji kara gogo goji made hatarakimasu.
10. Kanai to Nihon ni ikimashita.

C.

Bentuk Kamus Dictionary Form	Kemahuan (Negatif) Desire (Negative)
taizai suru	taizai shitakunai
kariru	karitakunai
hanasu	hanashitakunai
iku	ikitakunai
shiru	shiritakunai
isōgu	isōgitakunai
kurikaesu	kurikaeshitakunai
shimeru	shimetakunai
taberu	tabetakunai
nomu	nomitakunai

Daijūnika – Yūbinkyoku
Pelajaran 12 – Pejabat Pos
Lesson 12 – Post office

A.

1. Yūbinkyoku wa doko desu ka?
2. Jū en kitte o nijū mai kudasai.
3. Kono hagaki wa kyō okureba (okutara), Tōkyō ni itsu tsukimasu ka?
4. Watashi tachi wa kawase o okuru tame ni yūbinkyoku e (ni) ikimashita.
5. Anata wa yūbinkyoku e (ni) arukeba (aruite ittara) sanpun shika kakarimasen.
6. Watashi ga anata deshitara (dattara) koko wa hatarakimasen.
7. Kanojo wa kirei deshitara (kirekattara), kare wa kanojo to kekkon shimasu.
8. Anata wa koko kara ikanakattara, watashi wa nakimasu.
9. Tenki wa yokattara, yūbinkyoku ni aruite ikitai desu.

B.

1. Yūbinkyoku wa doko desu ka?
2. Kono tegami o dashitai desu ga, ikura desu ka?
3. Kono tegami o kakitome ni shite kudasai.
4. Koko ni sain shite kudasai.
5. Yūbinkyoku wa koko kara tōi desu ka?
6. Anata wa Tōkyō ni ittara, hagaki o katte kudasaimasen ka?
7. Ashita wa yasumi deshitara, Tōkyō ni ikimashyoo ka?

C.

Perkataan Words	Jika (bentuk) If (form)	Jika (bentuk negatif) If (Negative form)
tabemasu	tabetara	tabenakattara
okurimasu	okutara	okuranakattara
yasumimasu	yasundara	yasumanakattara

yomimasu	yondara	yomanakattara
naraimasu	naratara	narawanakattara
unten shimasu	unten shitara	unten shinakattara
desu	deshitara	nakattara
warui	warukattara	warukunakattara
yoi	yokattara	yokunakattara
tōi	tōkattara	tōkunakattara

Daijūsanka – Byōki
Pelajaran 13 – Penyakit
Lesson 13 – Sickness

A.

Isha: Dōnasai mashita ka?

Kanja: Kaze ga hikimashita. Atama mo itai desu.

Isha: (Anata wa) netsu ga chotto (shukoshi) arimasu. Kinō wa netsu ga arimashita ka?

Kanja: Shirimasen desu.

Isha: Memai ga shimasu ka?

Kanja: Hai, memai ga shimasu.

Isha wa Taionkei o motte kite kudasai.
kangofu
ni:

Kanja: Nando arimasu ka?

Isha: Sesshi sanju nana do desu.

Kanja: Kibun ga taihen warui desu kara, kusuri o kudasaimasen ka?

Isha: Kono kusuri o yonde kudasai.

Kanja: Dōmo arigato.

Isha: Odaijini.

B.

1. Tabako o suwanaide kudasai.
2. Ashita wa uchi e (ni) konaide kudasai.
3. Kono kusuri o nomanakattara moto byoki ni narimasu.
4. Anata wa yoku hatarakanakereba narimasen.
5. Anata wa kono shiken ga ukenakereba narimasen.

Daijūyonka – Kōtsū
Pelajaran 14 – Lalulintas
Lesson 14 – Traffic

A.
1. Rainen wa Tōkyō ni ikitai desu.
2. Dōshite ikimasu ka?
3. Tōkyō iki no kippu o (ichimai) kudasai.
4. 8 (hachi) gatsu 1 (tsuitachi) no kippu o kudasai.
5. Tsugi no eki wa doko desu ka?
6. Ginza ni chikatetsu de itta koto ga arimasu ka?
7. Takushii o yonde kudasai.
8. Kono kisha wa Ōsaka de tomarimasu ka?
9. Migi ni(e) magatte kudasai.
10. Hikōki ni noritai desu.

B.
1. Shita
2. Chiisai
3. Takusan
4. Bimbo
5. Tsukimasu
6. Hidari
7. Orimasu
8. Urimasu
9. Okimasu
10. Kimasu
11. Tachimasu
12. Kuroi
13. Demasu
14. Moraimasu
15. Takai
16. Samui
17. Atatakai
18. Hashirimasu
19. Joyū
20. Shimemasu

Daijugoka – Shushoku
Pelajaran 15 – Pekerjaan
Lesson 15 – Employment

A.
1. Kinō wa mensetsu ni ikimashita.
2. Doko no daigaku o sotsugyō shimashita ka?
3. Sotsugyō shite kara, nani o shimashita?
4. 3 (san) nenkan wa Nihongo no sensei ni narimashita.
5. Raishū no kinyōbi kara shigoto o hajimeru koto ga dekimasu ka?
6. Uchi ni kite mo, dame desu.
7. Shokuji wa takakutemo, taihen oishii deshita.
8. Kyō wa kyūryō ga morau koto ga dekimasu ka?

C.

Perkataan Words	Bolehkah anda Can You	Bentuk walaupun Even if (form)
sawarimasu	sawaru koto ga dekimasu	sawatte mo
tsukaimasu	tsukau koto ga dekimasu	tsukatte mo
ugokimasu	ugoku koto ga dekimasu	ugoite mo
nugimasu	nugu koto ga dekimasu	nuide mo
urimasu	uru koto ga dekimasu	utte mo
tachimasu	tatsu koto ga dekimasu	tatte mo
oyogimasu	oyogu koto ga dekimasu	oyonde mo
tabemasu	taberu koto ga dekimasu	tabete mo

Dai jūrokka – Fukushū
Pelajaran 16 – Latihan Ulangkaji
Lesson 16 – Review Exercises

A. *Isikan tempat-tempat kosong.*
Fill in the blanks.

Gantinama Pronouns	*Saya* I **Watashi**	*Kamu/Awak* You **Anata**	*Dia (Perempuan)* She **Kanojo**	*Dia (Laki-laki)* He **Kare**	*Kita* We **Watashi tachi**
Angka Numerals	2 **Ni** 0 **Rei**	4 **Shi, yon** 13 **Jūsan**	6 **Roku** 30 **Sanjū**	8 **Hachi** 101 **Hyaku ichi**	9 **Ku, kyū** 718 **Nanahyaku jūhachi**
Hari dalam minggu Days of the week	*Ahad* Sunday **Nichiyōbi**	*Selasa* Tuesday **Kayōbi**	*Rabu* Wednesday **Suiyōbi**	*Sabtu* Saturday **Doyōbi**	*Jumaat* Friday **Kinyōbi**
Warna Colour	*Merah* Red **Akai**	*Biru* Blue **Aoi**	*Hitam* Black **Kuroi**	*Kuning* Yellow **Kiiro**	*Putih* White **Shiroi**
	Kelabu Grey **Nezumiro**	*Hijau* Green **Midori**	*Ungu* Purple **Murasaki**	*Merah muda* Pink **Momoiro**	*Pelang* Brown **Chairo**

Haribulan Day of the month	*1hb* 1st **Tsuitachi**	*3hb* 3rd **Mikka**	*7hb* 7th **Nanoka**	*8hb* 8th **Yōka**	*9hb* 9th **Kokonoka**
Bulan Months	*20hb* 20th **Hatsuka**	*23hb* 23rd **Nijūsannichi**	*25hb* 25th **Nijūgonichi**	*30hb* 30th **Sanjunichi**	*31hb* 31st **Sanjūichinichi**
	Januari January **Ichigatsu**	*April* April **Shigatsu**	*Jun* June **Rokugatsu**	*Disember* December **Junigatsu**	*November* November **Jūichigatsu**
	Ogos August **Hachigatsu**	*September* September **Kugatsu**	*Februari* February **Nigatsu**	*Mac* March **Sangatsu**	*Juloi* July **Shichigatsu**
Proposisi (tempat) Location	*Di dalam* Inside **Naka**	*Atas* Top **Ue**	*Sebelah* Beside **Soba**	*Bawah* Under **Shita**	*Belakang* Behind **Ushiro**
	Depan Front **Mae**	*Di sini* Here **Koko**	*Di sana* There **Soko**	*Sebelah* Over there **Asoko**	*Sana* In **Ni**
	Di At **De**	*Mana* Where **Doko**	*Sebelah sana* Over there **Asoko**	*Jauh* Far **Tōi**	*Dekat* Near **Chikaku**
Anggota badan manusia Parts of the human body	*Kepala* Head **Atama**	*Perut* Stomach **I, Onaka**	*Gigi* Teeth **Ha**	*Tangan* Hand **Te**	*Kaki* Leg **Ashi**
	Mulut Mouth **Kuchi**	*Mata* Eyes **Me**	*Pergelangan kaki* Ankle **Kakato**	*Kerongkong* Throat **Nodo**	*Jari* Finger **Yubi**

	Paru-paru Lung **Hai**	*Gelembong* Bladder **Bōkō**	*Jantung* Heart **Shinzō**	*Usus* Intestines **Chō**	*Appendicitis* Appendicitis **Mochōen**	*Dada* Chest **Mune**
Pekerjaan Professions	*Doktor* Doctor **Isha**	*Peguam* Lawyer **Bengoshi**	*Jururawat* Nurse **Kangofu**	*Guru* Teacher **Sensei**	*Jurutera* Engineer **Gishi**	*Pelajar* Student **Gakusei**
	Pengurus Manager **Buchō**	*Ketua bahagian* Section chief **Kachō**	*Pekerja syarikat* Company workers **Shain**	*Pelakon (laki-laki)* Actor **Haiyū**	*Pelakon (wanita)* Actress **Joyū**	*Penyanyi* Singer **Kashu**
Keturunan Nationality	*Jepun* Japanese **Nihonjin**	*Malaysia* Malaysian **Marēshiajin**	*Singapura* Singaporean **Shingaporujin**	*Amerika* American **Amerikajin**	*German* German **Doitsujin**	*Belanda* Dutch **Orandajin**
Katakerja Verbs	*Makan* Eat **Tabemasu**	*Minum* Drink **Nomimasu**	*Bangun* Get up **Okimasu**	*Tidur* Sleep **Nemasu**	*Kerja* Work **Hatarakimasu**	*Rehat* Rest **Yasumimasu**
	Kahwin Marry **Kekkon shimasu**	*Pandu* Drive **Unten shimasu**	*Bersih* Clean **Sōji shimasu**	*Hantar* Send **Okurimasu**	*Kelahi* Quarrel **Kenka shimasu**	*Jumpa* Meet **Aimasu**
	Cakap Talk **Hanashimasu**	*Buka* Open **Akemasu**	*Tutup* Close **Shimemasu**	*Memasang suis* Switch on **Tsukimasu**	*Memadam suis* Switch off **Keshimasu**	*Duduk* Sit **Suwarimasu**
	Lihat See **Mimasu**	*Dengar* Listen **Kikimasu**	*Tulis* Write **Kakimasu**	*Berbau* To Smell **Kagimasu**	*Pertunangan* To get Engaged **Konyaku shimasu**	*Ambil* Take **Torimasu**

Adjektif / Adjectives	*Cantik* / Beautiful / **Kirei**	*Kecil* / Small / **Chiisai**	*Besar* / Big / **Ōkii**	*Murah* / Cheap / **Yasui**	*Mahal* / Expensive / **Takai**	*Keras* / Hard / **Katai**
	Lembut / Soft / **Yawarakai**	*Susah* / Difficult / **Muzukashii**	*Lebar* / Wide / **Hiroi**	*Sempit* / Narrow / **Semai**	*Gelap* / Dark / **Kurai**	*Terang* / Bright / **Akarui**
Adverba / Adverbs	*Berbagai* / Various / **Iroiro**	*Perlahan-lahan* / Slowly / **Yukkuri**	*Baik* / Well / **Yoku**	*Sedikit* / Little / **Shukoshi**	*Terbaik* / Best / **Ichiban**	*Sudah* / Already / **Mō**
	Serta-merta / At once / **Sugu**	*Selalu* / Always / **Itsumo**	*Hampir* / Almost / **Hotondo**	*Mungkin* / May be / **Tabun**	*Kadang-kadang* / Sometimes / **Tokidoki**	*Belum lagi* / Not yet / **Mada**
Peralatan / Stationery	*Pen* / Pen / **Pen**	*Kertas* / Paper / **Kami**	*Pensil* / Pencil / **Enpitsu**	*Buku surat* / Letter pad / **Binsen**	*Sampul surat* / Envelope / **Fūtō**	*Surat* / Letter / **Tegami**
Pakaian / Things to wear	*Baju* / Shirt / **Shatsu**	*Kasut* / Shoes / **Kutsu**	*Seluar* / Trousers / **Jubon**	*Topi* / Cap, Hat / **Bōshi**	*Pakaian* / Clothes / **Fuku**	*Sarong kaki* / Socks / **Kutsushita**
Cuaca, Musim / Weather, Seasons	*Panas* / Hot / **Atsui**	*Sejuk* / Cold / **Samui**	*Sejuk (dingin)* / Cool / **Suzushii**	*Panas* / Warm / **Atatakai**	*Angin* / Wind / **Kaze**	*Hujan* / Rain / **Ame**
	Salji / Snow / **Yuki**	*Musim bunga* / Spring / **Haru**	*Musim panas* / Summer / **Natsu**	*Musim gugur* / Autumn / **Aki**	*Musim dingin* / Winter / **Fuyu**	*Musim hujan* / Rainy season / **Uki**

	Berangin Windy **Kaze fuki**	Taufan Typhoon **Taifū**	Banjir Flood **Ōmizu**	Hujan renyai-renyai Light rain **Kosame**	Hujan lebat Heavy rain **Ōame**	Hari Baik Fine day **Hare**
Rasa Taste	*Sedap* Sweet **Amai**	*Masin* Salty **Karai**	*Masam* Sour **Suppai**	*Pahit* Bitter **Nigai**	*Berrempah* Spicy **Kosho karai**	*Lazat* Delicious **Oishii**

B. Dōshi
Verbs

Katakerja

Kata sekarang Present Tense	*Kata lampau* Past Tense	*Kata lampau negatif* Past Tense (Negative)	*Bentuk suruhan (halus)* Please (form)	*Bentuk suruhan negatif (halus)* Please (negative)
Tabemasu	**Tabemashita**	**Tabemasen deshita**	**Tabete kudasai**	**Tabenaide kudasai**
Urimasu	**Urimashita**	**Urimasen deshita**	**Utte kudasai**	**Uranaide kudasai**
Kaimasu	**Kaimashita**	**Kaimasen deshita**	**Katte kudasai**	**Kawanaide kudasai**
Okimasu	**Okimashita**	**Okimasen deshita**	**Okite kudasai**	**Okinaide kudasai**

Nemasu	Nemashita	Nemasen deshita	Nete kudasai	Nenaide kudasai
Kakimasu	Kakimashita	Kakimasen deshita	Kaite kudasai	Kakanaide kudasai
Nomimasu	Nomimashita	Nomimasen deshita	Nonde kudasai	Nomanaide kudasai
Hatarakimasu	Hatarakimashita	Hatarakimasen deshita	Hataraite kudasai	Hatarakanaide kudasai
Machimasu	Machimashita	Machimasen deshita	Matte kudasai	Matanaide kudasai
Kekkon shimasu	Kekkon shimashita	Kekkon shimasen deshita	Kekkon shite kudasai	Kekkon shinaide kudasai
Ryori shimasu	Ryori shimashita	Ryori shimasen deshita	Ryori shite kudasai	Ryori shinaide kudasai
Unten shimasu	Unten shimashita	Unten shimasen deshita	Unten shite kudasai	Unten shinaide kudasai
Moraimasu	Moraimashita	Moraimasen deshita	Morate kudasai	Morawanaide kudasai
Yomimasu	Yomimashita	Yomimasen deshita	Yonde kudasai	Yomanaide kudasai

Kata Sekarang Present Tense	Mesti Must	Jika If	Walaupun Even if	Keinginan Desire
Ikimasu	Ikanakereba narimasen	Ittara	Itte mo	Ikitai
Kimasu	Konakereba narimasen	Kitara	Kite mo	Kitai
Akemasu	Akenakereba narimasen	Aketara	Akete mo	Aketai
Shimemasu	Shimenakereba narimasen	Shimetara	Shimete mo	Shimetai
Torimasu	Toranakereba narimasen	Tottara	Totte mo	Toritai
Hanashimasu	Hanasanakereba narimasen	Hanashitara	Hanashite mo	Hanashitai
Sagashimasu	Sagasanakereba narimasen	Sagashitara	Sagashite mo	Sagashitai
Yasumimasu	Yasumanakereba narimasen	Yasundara	Yasunde mo	Yasumitai
Mimasu	Minakereba narimasen	Mitara	Mite mo	Mitai

Yamemasu	Yamenakereba narimasen	Yametara	Yamete mo	Yametai
Suzukemasu	Suzukenakereba narimasen	Suzuketara	Suzukete mo	Suzuketai
Unten shimasu	Untenshinakereba narimasen	Unten shitara	Unten shite mo	Unten shitai
Sōji shimasu	Sōji shinakereba narimasen	Sōji shitara	Sōji shite mo	Sōji shitai
Shinpai shimasu	Shinapaishina reba narimasen	Shinpai shitara	Shinpai shite mo	Shinpai shitai
Sanpo shimasu	Sanposhinake reba narimasen	Sanpo shitara	Sanpo shite mo	Sanpo shitai

D.
  (a) Kakimashita
  (b) Shimasu (kakemasu)
  (c) Itai desu
  (d) Sukimasu
  (e) Hikimashita
  (f) Futeimasu
  (g) Kakemasu
  (h) Yobimashita
  (i) Utte kudasai
  (j) Kaimashita

E.
  (a) Omedetō gōzaimasu.
  (b) Sumimasen.
  (c) Hajimemashita. Watashi wa _____ desu. Dōzo yoroshiku.
  (d) Ojama itashimashita.
  (e) Yukkuri hanashite kudasai.
  (f) Itadakimasu.
  (g) Gochiso sama deshita.
  (h) Isoide kudasai.
  (i) Omatase shimashita.
  (j) Sayōnara.
  (k) Masugu itte kudasai.
  (l) Migi e (ni) magatte kudasai.
  (m) Doko ni sundeimasu ka?
  (n) Koko wa doko desu ka?
  (o) Ikura desu ka?
  (p) Takushii o yonde kudasai.

F.
  (a) Kono michi wa Shingapōru ni ikimasu ka?
  (b) Kono heya wa (ga) semai desu.
  (c) Tōkyō wa Ōsaka yori ōkii desu.
  (d) Gin wa kin yori takaku wa arimasen.
  (e) Gogo niji jūppun sugi ni kite kudasai.
  (f) Nanji ni kaete kimasu ka?

(g) Hon o (koko wa) motte kite kudasi.

(h) Yūbinkyoku e (ni) kozutsumi o okuru (tame) ni ikimashita.

(i) "Blue" wa Nihongo de nan to iimasu ka?

(j) Okane wa nakattara (mottanakattara), nani mo kau koto dekimasen.

(k) Jidōsha (kuruma) de juppun gurai kakarimasu.

(l) Yukkuri hanashite mo, (watashi wa) wakaru koto ga dekimasen.

(m) Denwa de yoyaku o suru koto ga dekimasu.

Daijūshichika — Dōshi
Pelajaran 17 — Katakerja
Lesson 17 — Verbs

A.

1. Tabeteiru
2. Nondeiru
3. Tabeta
4. Okiteiru
5. Miteiru
6. Kiita
7. Suwaranakatta
8. Tattanakatta
9. Unten shinai
10. Kekkon shinai
11. Katta
12. Utta
13. Kazoeru
14. Kazoenakatta
15. Okuranakuccha
16. Ikanakuccha
17. Yomanakuccha
18. Oboeru
19. Omou
20. Aruku

B.

Bentuk kamus Dictionary Form	Kata lampau Past Tense	Kata lampau (negatif) Past Negative	Kata sekarang (negatif) Present Negative	Kata sekarang (berterusan) Present Continuous	Kata lampau (berterusan) Past Continuous	Harus (mesti) Must
Aruku	Aruita	Arukanakatta	Arukanai	Aruiteiru	Aruiteitta	Arukanakuccha
Shimeru	Shimeta	Shimenakatta	Shimenai	Shimeteiru	Shimeteitta	Shimenakuccha
Taberu	Tabeta	Tabenakatta	Tabenai	Tabeteiru	Tabeteitta	Tabenakuccha
Hakobu	Hakcnda	Hakobanakatta	Hakobanai	Hakondeiru	Hakondeitta	Hakobanakuccha
Suwaru	Suwata	Suwaranakatta	Suwaranai	Suwateiru	Suwateitta	Suwarnakuccha
Sōji suru	Sōji shita	Sōji shinakatta	Sōji shinai	Sōji shiteiru	Sōji shiteitta	Sōji shinakuccha
Kuru	Kita	Konakatta	Konai	Kitteiru	Kiteitta	Konakuccha
Hanasu	Hanashita	Hanasanakatta	Hanasanai	Hanashiteiru	Hanashiteitta	Hanasanakuccha
Shiru	Shita	Shiranakatta	Shiranai	Shiteiru	Shiteitta	Shiranakuccha
Sanpo suru	Sanpo shita	Sanpo shinakatta	Sanpo shinai	Sanpo shiteiru	Sanpo shiteitta	Sanpo shinakuccha

Daijūhakka — Fukushi, Keiyōshi
Pelajaran 18 — Adverba, Adjektif
Lesson 18 — Adverbs, Adjectives

A.

(a) Mezurashiku
(b) Mada
(c) Saigo
(d) Hayaku
(e) Kitto
(f) Chiisai
(g) Takai
(h) Semai
(i) Suppai
(j) Atsui
(k) Atatakai
(l) Hayai
(m) Minikui
(n) Nagai
(o) Chikai (chikaku)
(p) Mazui
(q) Sawagashii (yakamashii)
(r) Tsumaranai
(s) Karui
(t) Atarashii

A classic work on the Malay language
by Pelanduk Publications

Malay for Everyone

By Othman Sulaiman

This is a specially designed teach-yourself book for those who are conversant in English and want to learn and master the Malay language, in the shortest possible time, in the privacy and comfort of their homes, at their own leisure.

Malay, or 'Bahasa Malaysia' as it is now known in Malaysia, has a rich history rivalling that of many European languages. During the Middle Ages in Europe, Malay Rulers spoke an increasingly refined 'Classical Malay' which had developed over the centuries from the cruder bazaar Malay of the archipelago's traders. In the 1400s' by the time the Malacca sultanate had been set up, epics such as the Malay Annals achieved a style and elegance second to none.

During the colonial era Classical Malay almost disappeared when the elite began to adopt the language of the colonial rulers. However, bazaar Malay survived among traders and ordinary folk and it was this language, together with a renewed interest in Classical Malay, which formed the basis of the National Language (Bahasa Malaysia or Malay) after Malaysia's independence in 1957. Since then Malay has been enriched by the addition of a wide range of new words and expressions consistent with its development as a language of modern technology. Moreover, cooperation with Indonesia, which also adopted Malay as its national language, has resulted in greater standardisation of spelling and terminology. Today, the language is known and used by more than 150 million Asians.

This book guarantees a thorough grounding of the Malay language in all the basic elements needed to secure a polished and full command of the language. This is not a dull and dry conventional coursebook, the lessons having been methodically prepared to ensure a rapid acquisition of Malay.